CALEB ROSS

C++ For Concurrency And Parallel Programming

Efficient Techniques for Multithreaded and Parallel Systems

Copyright © 2024 by Caleb Ross

All rights reserved. No part of this publication may be reproduced, stored or transmitted in any form or by any means, electronic, mechanical, photocopying, recording, scanning, or otherwise without written permission from the publisher. It is illegal to copy this book, post it to a website, or distribute it by any other means without permission.

First edition

This book was professionally typeset on Reedsy. Find out more at reedsy.com

Contents

Introduction: The Need for Concurrency and Parallelism in...	1
Chapter 1: Understanding Concurrency and Parallelism	7
Chapter 2: C++ Concurrency Basics	18
Chapter 3: Synchronization in C++	32
Chapter 4: Thread Synchronization Mechanisms in C++	46
Chapter 5: Advanced Thread Management in C++	57
Chapter 6: Designing Patterns for Concurrency in C++	67
Chapter 7: Real-World Applications of C++ Concurrency	77
Chapter 8: Advanced Topics in C++ Concurrency	89
Chapter 9: Case Studies and Real-World Examples in C++...	100
Chapter 10: Final Thoughts on C++ Concurrency	116
Chapter 11: Best Practices and Design Guidelines for C++...	122
Chapter 12: The Future of Concurrency in C++	132
Chapter 13: Reflections and Future Directions in C++...	139
Chapter 14: Case Studies and Applications of C++ Concurrency	146
Chapter 15: Final Reflections and the Future of C++...	161
Conclusion	169

Introduction: The Need for Concurrency and Parallelism in Modern Applications

The Evolution of Multithreading and Parallel Programming
Over the past few decades, computing power has expanded at an unprecedented rate. In the early days, computers were single-core machines, and the primary focus was on improving clock speeds to increase performance. However, by the early 2000s, a new problem emerged: increasing clock speeds was no longer a viable method for improving performance due to physical limitations, such as heat dissipation and power consumption. As a result, the industry shifted from increasing clock speeds to increasing the number of cores in a processor.

This transition marked the dawn of **multicore processors**, where several independent cores could handle different tasks simultaneously. To fully utilize these cores, **multithreading** and **parallel programming** became essential.

Multithreading refers to the ability of a program to manage multiple threads (smaller units of a process) concurrently. Each thread can run independently and share resources like memory, but managing them efficiently becomes a challenge. Early implementations of multithreading were relatively simple, focusing on basic threading primitives like mutexes and semaphores to synchronize access to shared resources.

As software complexity increased, so did the demand for more efficient parallel processing techniques. The era of **parallel programming** was born, where tasks could not only be run concurrently (multithreading) but also broken down into smaller, independent sub-tasks to be executed in parallel, significantly reducing execution time and boosting performance.

Parallel programming involves splitting a task into smaller chunks that can be processed simultaneously by multiple cores, and then combining the results. This paradigm became crucial in domains like scientific computing, financial modeling, gaming, and artificial intelligence, where time-sensitive and resource-intensive operations demand high throughput and minimal latency.

As the hardware evolved, programming languages like C++ had to adapt to this paradigm shift. The rise of multicore processors brought with it new complexities. Writing multithreaded and parallel code is difficult because you must manage **concurrency**, **race conditions**, **deadlocks**, and **memory consistency**. Early solutions often relied on libraries and platform-specific solutions, but as the need grew, C++ evolved to provide native support for concurrency and parallelism. Today, with modern C++ standards, developers have access to a comprehensive set of tools for writing concurrent and parallel code efficiently.

Why Concurrency and Parallelism Matter

Concurrency and parallelism are crucial for modern software development, particularly in a world where we increasingly rely on multicore processors. Understanding the importance of concurrency and parallelism is fundamental to building high-performance, scalable applications. Let's break down why they matter.

1. **Performance and Scalability**
2. Concurrency and parallelism enable software to run faster and more efficiently on multicore processors. By dividing a task into smaller, independent subtasks, we can distribute the workload across multiple cores, leading to a significant reduction in overall execution time.
3. For example, consider an application that processes large datasets. If the application is written to run on a single core, it processes the data

sequentially. But by employing parallelism, the same task can be divided among multiple cores, allowing different parts of the dataset to be processed simultaneously. This leads to massive performance gains, particularly when working with computationally expensive tasks like simulations, image processing, or machine learning algorithms.

4. **Responsiveness in Real-Time Applications**
5. Concurrency allows applications to remain responsive, even when performing long-running operations. Imagine you're developing a video game or a real-time financial trading platform. These systems cannot afford to freeze or become unresponsive while processing large amounts of data or running complex algorithms in the background.
6. Concurrency solves this problem by enabling the system to manage multiple operations simultaneously. For instance, in a game, the logic for processing player movements, physics calculations, and rendering can run concurrently, ensuring smooth gameplay.
7. **Efficient Resource Utilization**
8. Modern systems are equipped with powerful multicore processors, but without proper multithreading and parallel programming, these cores remain underutilized. Efficient concurrency allows applications to make full use of the available hardware resources.
9. Single-threaded applications can bottleneck performance as they only utilize one core, while the other cores sit idle. Multithreading enables better distribution of tasks across cores, improving resource utilization and overall system efficiency.
10. **Handling I/O Bound Tasks**
11. In many applications, a significant portion of time is spent waiting for I/O operations like reading from disk or making network requests. These tasks are generally slow and can block the execution of other operations, leading to inefficiencies. By employing concurrency, such tasks can be offloaded to background threads, allowing the main application to continue processing without waiting for I/O-bound tasks to complete.
12. For example, a web server can handle multiple requests concurrently,

improving its responsiveness and scalability, even when some requests involve slow database queries or file operations.
13. **Parallelizing Complex Calculations**
14. Some applications, especially those in the fields of scientific computing, financial modeling, or machine learning, involve complex calculations that can be time-consuming when run sequentially. Parallelism can significantly speed up these calculations by dividing the problem into smaller sub-problems and solving them concurrently.
15. For instance, a matrix multiplication operation, which is common in machine learning, can be parallelized by splitting the matrix into smaller blocks and distributing the calculations across multiple cores. This reduces computation time, allowing the system to process large datasets efficiently.
16. **Meeting the Demands of High-Throughput Systems**
17. Many modern systems need to process a large number of requests or transactions per second, such as in web servers, database systems, or cloud-based services. Concurrency and parallelism are essential for meeting the performance and scalability requirements of such systems.
18. High-throughput systems can handle thousands of requests concurrently by distributing the workload across multiple threads or processes. This enables the system to serve a large number of users without sacrificing performance or responsiveness.
19. **Real-Time Data Processing**
20. With the rise of technologies like big data and real-time analytics, the ability to process data streams concurrently has become crucial. Systems need to process and analyze data as it arrives, often from multiple sources, in real-time. This requires efficient concurrency and parallelism strategies to ensure that the system can handle large volumes of data without falling behind.
21. For example, in a real-time fraud detection system, incoming transactions must be analyzed and processed immediately. Any delay in processing could result in fraudulent activity going unnoticed. By leveraging parallel processing, such systems can handle multiple data

streams simultaneously, ensuring timely and accurate results.

Overview of C++ Concurrency Support

C++ is one of the most widely used programming languages in the world, and its support for concurrency has evolved significantly over the years. With the introduction of **C++11**, the language gained built-in support for concurrency through the **C++ Standard Library**, providing tools for multithreading, synchronization, and parallelism. Since then, newer versions of C++ (such as C++14, C++17, and C++20) have added even more powerful features for writing concurrent and parallel programs.

Here's an overview of some of the most important concurrency features in modern C++:

1. **std::thread: Native Thread Support**
2. Prior to C++11, developers had to rely on platform-specific libraries like POSIX threads (on Unix-based systems) or the Windows API for multithreading. C++11 introduced std::thread, a standard, cross-platform way to create and manage threads.
3. The std::thread class provides a simple interface for creating threads and handling their lifecycle. It allows developers to spawn new threads and execute functions in parallel. Threads can be joined (waiting for them to complete) or detached (allowing them to run independently).
4. **Mutexes and Locks for Synchronization**
5. One of the biggest challenges in multithreading is coordinating access to shared resources. If multiple threads try to modify the same data simultaneously, it can lead to race conditions, where the final outcome depends on the timing of thread execution. To prevent this, C++ provides **mutexes** (std::mutex), which are used to lock resources, ensuring that only one thread can access them at a time.
6. Additionally, C++ offers **lock guards** (std::lock_guard and std::unique_lock) to simplify the management of locks and ensure that they are released correctly when no longer needed.
7. **Condition Variables for Thread Communication**

8. Sometimes, threads need to communicate with each other, for example, when one thread is waiting for another to finish processing. **Condition variables** (std::condition_variable) provide a way for threads to notify each other and wait for certain conditions to be met.
9. Condition variables allow threads to pause execution until a specific event occurs, at which point they can be signaled to resume. This is particularly useful in scenarios where one thread needs to wait for data from another before continuing.
10. **Futures and Promises for Asynchronous Programming**
11. Asynchronous programming involves performing tasks in the background while allowing the main program to continue executing. C++ provides **futures** (std::future) and **promises** (std::promise) for handling asynchronous tasks and retrieving results once they are available.
12. Futures represent the result of an asynchronous computation, while promises are used to set the value of the future. Additionally, std::async allows developers to run tasks asynchronously and retrieve the result using a future.
13. **Atomic Operations for Lock-Free Programming**
14. In high-performance systems, locking can introduce significant overhead, especially when contention between threads is high. C++ provides **atomic operations** (std::atomic) that allow for lock-free programming, where threads can operate on shared data without requiring explicit locks.
15. Atomic operations are crucial for building lock-free data structures and algorithms, which can significantly improve performance in multi thread.

Chapter 1: Understanding Concurrency and Parallelism

Concurrency vs. Parallelism: Key Differences

The concepts of **concurrency** and **parallelism** are often confused or used interchangeably, but they represent distinct approaches to handling multiple tasks in computing. Understanding the difference between them is crucial to developing efficient, scalable, and high-performance applications.

1. **Concurrency**
2. Concurrency refers to the ability of a system to manage multiple tasks at once, even though they might not be running simultaneously. In a concurrent system, multiple tasks can make progress over time, but they may be interleaved rather than executed at the same instant. Think of concurrency as time-sharing: different tasks are allocated slices of time on the processor, with the illusion that they are running simultaneously, even though the tasks are often paused and resumed in sequence.
3. **Concurrency is about structure.** It's more focused on enabling multiple tasks to exist and be managed at once, but not necessarily run at the same time. Concurrency is beneficial for maintaining responsiveness in programs, especially when performing input/output (I/O) operations or interacting with external systems like databases or network requests.

For example, while one part of a program is waiting for data to be retrieved from a database, another part of the program can continue processing other tasks.
4. **Example**:
5. Imagine you're using a web browser. You might have several tabs open, each loading different websites. Even though your computer has a single CPU core, the browser switches between these tabs, loading parts of each website as resources become available. This switching is an example of concurrency. Multiple tasks (loading web pages) are in progress, but they aren't necessarily happening at the same time. Concurrency helps the browser manage all tasks without making it unresponsive.
6. **Parallelism**
7. Parallelism, on the other hand, involves running multiple tasks at the same time. In a parallel system, multiple tasks are executed simultaneously across multiple cores or processors. Parallelism takes full advantage of modern multicore processors by distributing tasks so that different parts of a problem are processed at the same time.
8. **Parallelism is about execution**. It's focused on increasing the throughput of a system by running multiple tasks in parallel. For this to happen, the tasks need to be independent of each other so that they can run simultaneously without interfering. Parallelism can significantly improve performance in tasks that require heavy computation, such as matrix multiplication, data analysis, and image processing.
9. **Example**:
10. Consider a factory assembly line. Different workers (or robots) perform various tasks on different parts of the product at the same time. One worker might be assembling the frame, while another is installing the engine, and another is adding the electronics. Each worker is doing their task simultaneously, allowing the product to be completed faster. This is parallelism — multiple tasks are running in parallel to achieve a faster outcome.
11. **Concurrency vs. Parallelism in Practice**
12. The fundamental difference between concurrency and parallelism lies

in their goals: concurrency focuses on managing multiple tasks that can interleave over time, while parallelism is about performing many tasks simultaneously. It's important to note that a system can be concurrent without being parallel (if the tasks are interleaved rather than executed at the same time), and it can be parallel without being concurrent (if tasks are executed simultaneously but don't involve any switching or interleaving).
13. **Concurrency** is useful in situations where tasks spend a lot of time waiting (e.g., for I/O operations), while **parallelism** is beneficial for tasks that are computationally intensive and can be broken down into independent units. Both approaches are essential in modern computing, especially in multicore systems where concurrency manages the flow of multiple tasks, and parallelism improves throughput by distributing tasks across available cores.
14. **Use Case Comparison**:

- **Concurrency**: A single-core processor switching between tasks like fetching data from a server, processing it, and updating the UI. Each task might not be running at the same time, but they all progress as the processor switches between them.
- **Parallelism**: A multicore processor performing complex calculations, such as rendering a 3D scene, where different parts of the image are rendered in parallel by different cores.

The Importance of Multithreading in Performance Optimization

Multithreading is the ability of a CPU (or a program) to execute multiple threads simultaneously. In modern computing, multithreading is a critical technique for optimizing performance, especially on multicore processors, where several tasks can be executed in parallel to improve efficiency and reduce execution time.

1. **Understanding Threads**
2. A thread is the smallest unit of processing that can be scheduled by an

operating system. In a single-threaded application, the program executes one instruction after another in a sequential manner. However, in a multithreaded application, multiple threads are created, and each thread runs a part of the program independently.

3. **Example**:
4. In a video game, one thread might handle the game's physics calculations, another might manage rendering the graphics, and yet another might process user input. By splitting these tasks into different threads, the game can maintain smooth and responsive performance, even during complex operations like rendering large scenes or handling multiple inputs simultaneously.
5. **Benefits of Multithreading**

- **Improved Responsiveness**: Multithreading allows applications to remain responsive while performing long-running tasks. For example, in a user interface application, the main thread can handle user input while background threads process data or perform network operations. This ensures that the application doesn't freeze while waiting for slow operations to complete.
- **Efficient Resource Utilization**: On a multicore system, multithreading enables better utilization of the available CPU cores. By distributing tasks across multiple threads, the workload can be spread across different cores, maximizing CPU usage and improving overall performance.
- **Faster Execution of Complex Tasks**: Tasks that can be divided into smaller, independent subtasks benefit significantly from multithreading. For instance, in data processing or simulation applications, multithreading allows different parts of the dataset to be processed simultaneously, reducing the total execution time.
- **Concurrency in I/O-Bound Tasks**: Multithreading is especially useful in applications where tasks spend a lot of time waiting for I/O operations, such as file reading/writing or network communication. By offloading these tasks to background threads, the main application can continue executing other tasks without waiting for the I/O operations to complete.

CHAPTER 1: UNDERSTANDING CONCURRENCY AND PARALLELISM

1. **Challenges in Multithreading**
2. While multithreading offers significant performance improvements, it also introduces challenges that developers must address to ensure correct and efficient execution.

- **Synchronization Issues**: When multiple threads access shared resources, such as memory or data structures, they must be properly synchronized to prevent race conditions, where the outcome depends on the timing of thread execution. Synchronization mechanisms like mutexes and locks are used to ensure that only one thread accesses a shared resource at a time, but they can introduce overhead and cause performance bottlenecks if not managed efficiently.
- **Deadlocks**: A deadlock occurs when two or more threads are waiting for each other to release resources, causing them to block indefinitely. Avoiding deadlocks requires careful design of the program's threading model, ensuring that resources are acquired and released in a consistent order.
- **Thread Overhead**: Creating and managing threads comes with overhead. While threads can improve performance by allowing tasks to run concurrently, creating too many threads can lead to excessive context switching (the process of saving and restoring thread states), which can degrade performance. Balancing the number of threads to the available CPU resources is critical for achieving optimal performance.

1. **Multithreading in C++**
2. C++ provides built-in support for multithreading through the **C++ Standard Library**, which includes the std::thread class for creating and managing threads. C++ also offers synchronization primitives like mutexes, condition variables, and atomic operations to manage access to shared resources and ensure thread safety.
3. **Example**:
4. In C++, creating a new thread is as simple as calling the std::thread constructor with a function or callable object. The thread will execute

the function in parallel with the main thread, allowing multiple tasks to be executed concurrently.

```cpp
Copy code
#include <iostream>
#include <thread>

void printMessage() {
    std::cout << "Hello from a thread!" << std::endl;
}

int main() {
    std::thread t(printMessage);
    t.join();   // Wait for the thread to finish
    return 0;
}
```

1. In this example, the printMessage function is executed in a separate thread, running concurrently with the main program. The join() function ensures that the main thread waits for the new thread to finish before continuing.

Asynchronous Programming vs. Synchronous Execution

In software development, understanding the difference between **asynchronous programming** and **synchronous execution** is key to building efficient, responsive applications, especially when dealing with I/O-bound tasks, network operations, or background processing.

1. **Synchronous Execution**
2. In a synchronous program, tasks are executed sequentially, one after the other. Each task must complete before the next one can begin. While this approach is straightforward and easy to understand, it can lead to inefficiencies, particularly when tasks involve waiting for I/O operations

CHAPTER 1: UNDERSTANDING CONCURRENCY AND PARALLELISM

or external resources.
3. **Example**:
4. Consider a program that needs to download a file from a remote server and then process the file's contents. In a synchronous program, the download operation would block the entire program until the file has been fully retrieved. Only after the download is complete would the program begin processing the file. This means that the program is idle during the time it waits for the network operation to complete, which can lead to wasted CPU cycles and reduced performance.
5. **Asynchronous Programming**
6. Asynchronous programming allows tasks to be performed in the background without blocking the main thread. In an asynchronous program, the main thread initiates a task, such as downloading a file, and then immediately continues executing other tasks while the download is handled in the background. When the download is complete, the program can be notified (usually via a callback or a future/promise mechanism) and proceed with processing the file.
7. **Example**:
8. In the same file download scenario, an asynchronous approach would allow the program to initiate the download and then continue executing other tasks, such as updating the user interface or handling user input, without waiting for the download to complete. Once the download finishes, the program is notified, and the file can be processed.
9. **Asynchronous programming improves responsiveness** in applications that deal with I/O-bound tasks. It allows the program to remain responsive to user input and other tasks, even when waiting for external resources.
10. **Asynchronous Programming in C++**
11. C++ provides built-in support for asynchronous programming through the **std::future** and **std::async** mechanisms. These tools allow developers to run tasks asynchronously and retrieve the result at a later time, once the task has completed.

```cpp
Copy code
#include <iostream>
#include <future>

int downloadFile() {
    // Simulate a file download
    std::this_thread::sleep_for(std::chrono::seconds(3));
    return 42;  // Download result
}

int main() {
    // Launch an asynchronous task
    std::future<int> result = std::async(downloadFile);

    std::cout << "Doing other work while the file is
    downloading..." << std::endl;

    // Get the result of the download (blocks until the download
    is complete)
    int fileResult = result.get();
    std::cout << "File download completed with result: " <<
    fileResult << std::endl;

    return 0;
}
```

1. In this example, the downloadFile function simulates a file download, but instead of blocking the main thread, it runs asynchronously using std::async. The main thread continues executing while the download is in progress, and the result is retrieved later using the future.get() method.
2. **Synchronous vs. Asynchronous Use Cases**

- **Synchronous Execution**: Best suited for tasks that must be performed sequentially or when the overhead of managing asynchronous tasks is not justified. For example, in simple programs where tasks do not involve

long waiting periods, synchronous execution might be the simplest and most efficient approach.
- **Asynchronous Programming**: Ideal for tasks that involve waiting for I/O operations, network requests, or other external resources. Asynchronous programming keeps the application responsive, even when dealing with long-running operations.

1. **Common Use Cases for Asynchronous Programming**:

- Network communication (e.g., HTTP requests, WebSockets)
- File I/O operations (e.g., reading/writing large files)
- User interface applications that must remain responsive while performing background tasks
- Server applications that handle multiple client requests concurrently

Real-World Applications of Concurrency

Concurrency is widely used in modern software applications to improve performance, scalability, and responsiveness. Some of the key areas where concurrency plays a critical role include:

1. **Web Servers and Cloud-Based Services**
2. Web servers handle multiple client requests simultaneously. Concurrency allows the server to process requests from multiple users at once, without making any user wait for the server to finish processing another user's request.
3. In cloud-based services, concurrency is essential for handling a large number of simultaneous operations, such as serving web pages, processing transactions, or managing data storage.
4. **Example**:
5. A modern web server, such as Nginx or Apache, uses multithreading and asynchronous I/O to handle thousands of client connections concurrently. This ensures that users experience minimal latency, even when the server is handling a high volume of traffic.

6. **Real-Time Systems**
7. Real-time systems, such as those used in aviation, medical devices, and automotive systems, rely heavily on concurrency to meet strict timing requirements. These systems must process multiple tasks concurrently while ensuring that critical tasks meet their deadlines.
8. **Example**:
9. In a flight control system, concurrency is used to manage tasks such as monitoring the aircraft's sensors, adjusting flight controls, and communicating with ground control. Each of these tasks must run concurrently to ensure the safe operation of the aircraft.
10. **Gaming and Simulation**
11. In gaming, concurrency is used to handle multiple tasks simultaneously, such as rendering graphics, processing player input, and simulating physics. By using concurrency, game developers can ensure smooth gameplay and responsiveness, even in complex environments with many moving parts.
12. **Example**:
13. In a multiplayer online game, concurrency is used to manage multiple players' actions in real-time, ensuring that the game world remains synchronized for all players.
14. **Big Data and Machine Learning**
15. In data processing and machine learning, concurrency is used to handle large datasets efficiently. By processing data in parallel, systems can analyze and extract insights from massive datasets in a fraction of the time it would take using a single-threaded approach.
16. **Example**:
17. In a machine learning pipeline, concurrency is used to train models on large datasets, where different parts of the dataset are processed simultaneously to speed up the training process.
18. **Financial Systems**
19. Financial systems, such as stock trading platforms, rely on concurrency to handle real-time market data and execute trades. These systems must process a large number of transactions and data feeds concurrently

to ensure that traders have the most up-to-date information and can execute trades with minimal delay.
20. **Example**:
21. A high-frequency trading system uses concurrency to process market data feeds, execute trades, and manage risk calculations, all in real-time.

Chapter 2: C++ Concurrency Basics

Concurrency is one of the most important features in modern C++, especially with the increasing demand for high-performance, scalable applications. C++ provides a rich set of tools to handle concurrency, making it easier for developers to take advantage of multicore systems. One of the foundational components for writing concurrent programs in C++ is std::thread, introduced in C++11, which allows developers to create and manage threads efficiently.

In this chapter, we will explore the basic concepts of multithreading in C++, focusing on std::thread, thread creation and management, thread lifecycle, and common pitfalls in multithreading. By understanding these concepts, you will be able to write efficient multithreaded applications that can utilize the full power of modern hardware.

Introduction to std::thread

In C++, a thread is an independent path of execution within a program. Threads allow you to perform multiple tasks concurrently, which can lead to significant performance improvements, especially on systems with multiple cores. Prior to C++11, developers had to rely on platform-specific libraries like POSIX threads (on Unix-based systems) or the Windows API to create and manage threads. This made writing cross-platform multithreaded code cumbersome and error-prone.

With the introduction of the std::thread class in C++11, multithreading became part of the C++ Standard Library, offering a cross-platform way to manage threads. The std::thread class provides an abstraction over the low-level threading primitives, making it easier to create and manage threads without worrying about the underlying system details.

Basic Usage of std::thread

To create a new thread in C++, you simply instantiate a std::thread object and pass it a callable object, such as a function, lambda expression, or function object. The new thread will execute the callable in parallel with the main thread.

Example:

```cpp
Copy code
#include <iostream>
#include <thread>

void printMessage() {
    std::cout << "Hello from the thread!" << std::endl;
}

int main() {
    std::thread t(printMessage);   // Create a new thread
    t.join();   // Wait for the thread to finish
    return 0;
}
```

In this example, the printMessage function is executed in a separate thread. The std::thread constructor is called with printMessage as its argument, which causes the function to be executed in parallel with the main thread. The join() method ensures that the main thread waits for the new thread to finish before continuing.

Thread Functions: Passing Arguments

Threads in C++ can take arguments just like normal functions. You can pass arguments to a thread by providing additional arguments to the std::thread constructor.

Example:

```cpp
Copy code
#include <iostream>
#include <thread>

void printNumber(int num) {
    std::cout << "Number: " << num << std::endl;
}

int main() {
    std::thread t(printNumber, 42);  // Pass the argument 42 to the thread
    t.join();
    return 0;
}
```

In this example, the printNumber function takes an integer argument. When creating the thread, we pass the number 42 as an argument to the std::thread constructor, which is forwarded to the printNumber function.

If you need to pass more complex objects, such as classes or structures, to a thread, C++ provides mechanisms like **move semantics** to efficiently pass large objects by avoiding unnecessary copies.

Lambda Expressions with std::thread

Lambda expressions are an excellent way to pass anonymous functions to threads. This is especially useful when you want to define the thread's behavior inline without creating a separate function.

Example:

```cpp
Copy code
#include <iostream>
#include <thread>

int main() {
```

```cpp
    std::thread t([] {
        std::cout << "Hello from the lambda thread!" << std::endl;
    });
    t.join();
    return 0;
}
```

In this example, a lambda expression is passed directly to the std::thread constructor. This approach can be very convenient for short, self-contained tasks.

Multithreading in Action: A Simple Example

Let's look at a more complex example where we create multiple threads to perform some computation concurrently.

Example:

```cpp
Copy code
#include <iostream>
#include <thread>
#include <vector>

void compute(int id) {
    std::cout << "Thread " << id << " is computing..." <<
    std::endl;
    // Simulate some work with a sleep
    std::this_thread::sleep_for(std::chrono::seconds(1));
    std::cout << "Thread " << id << " finished." << std::endl;
}

int main() {
    const int numThreads = 5;
    std::vector<std::thread> threads;

    // Create multiple threads
    for (int i = 0; i < numThreads; ++i) {
        threads.push_back(std::thread(compute, i));
    }
```

```
    // Wait for all threads to finish
    for (auto& t : threads) {
        t.join();
    }

    return 0;
}
```

This example creates five threads, each executing the compute function with a unique thread ID. The main thread waits for all the worker threads to complete by calling join() on each thread. This pattern of creating multiple threads to perform parallel tasks is common in multithreaded applications.

Thread Creation and Management

Creating and managing threads efficiently is critical to building scalable and performant applications. In C++, managing threads involves handling their lifecycle, ensuring proper synchronization, and preventing common issues like race conditions and deadlocks. Let's dive into the different aspects of thread management in C++.

Creating Threads

As we've seen, creating threads in C++ is straightforward using the std::thread class. When you instantiate a std::thread object, a new thread is created, and the callable passed to the constructor is executed concurrently.

However, there are a few key considerations when creating threads:

- **Thread Safety**: Ensure that any shared resources accessed by multiple threads are properly synchronized to prevent race conditions.
- **Thread Count**: Over-creating threads can lead to excessive context switching, which degrades performance. It's essential to balance the number of threads with the available hardware resources (e.g., CPU cores).

Joining Threads

One of the most important aspects of thread management is ensuring that threads complete their execution. The join() method is used to block the calling thread (typically the main thread) until the thread finishes execution. This is crucial when the main thread needs to wait for other threads to complete before continuing.

Example:

```cpp
Copy code
std::thread t(doWork);
t.join();  // Wait for the thread to finish before proceeding
```

Failure to call join() on a thread before the program exits can result in a crash, as the thread may still be running when the main thread terminates.

Detaching Threads

In some cases, you may want a thread to run independently of the main thread. For example, a background task like logging or monitoring doesn't need to block the main program. In such scenarios, you can use the detach() method, which allows the thread to run in the background without needing to be joined.

Example:

```cpp
Copy code
std::thread t(backgroundTask);
t.detach();  // Let the thread run independently
```

When a thread is detached, it runs independently and is no longer associated with the thread object. Once detached, the thread cannot be joined, and it becomes the responsibility of the operating system to clean up its resources when it finishes execution.

However, detaching a thread comes with risks. Since the main thread has no way of knowing when a detached thread finishes, accessing shared resources from a detached thread can lead to undefined behavior if those resources are deallocated before the detached thread completes.

Thread Lifecycle: Starting, Joining, and Detaching Threads

Understanding the lifecycle of a thread is essential to managing multi-threaded applications efficiently. The thread lifecycle consists of several stages:

1. **Creation**: A thread is created when a std::thread object is instantiated. At this point, the thread is in the **new** state and will soon begin executing the callable passed to it.
2. **Running**: Once the thread starts executing the callable, it is in the **running** state. The thread continues to execute its task independently of other threads.
3. **Blocking**: A thread may enter a **blocked** state if it is waiting for a resource, such as a lock or a condition variable. When the resource becomes available, the thread resumes execution.
4. **Joining or Detaching**: A thread can be joined by the main thread using the join() method. This causes the main thread to wait until the thread finishes execution. Alternatively, the thread can be detached using detach(), allowing it to run independently.
5. **Termination**: A thread terminates when it finishes executing its callable. If the thread is joined, the main thread continues execution. If the thread is detached, the operating system cleans up its resources when it finishes.

Thread Completion and Resource Cleanup

Proper thread management includes ensuring that all threads complete their execution and that resources are cleaned up properly. In C++, when a thread is joined, its resources are released, and it is marked as completed. Similarly, detached threads are cleaned up by the operating system after they finish.

One important aspect to note is that a std::thread object is **non-copyable**. Attempting to copy a thread object will result in a compilation error. However, std::thread objects are **movable**, meaning they can be transferred between variables using move semantics.

Example:

```cpp
Copy code
std::thread t1(doWork);
std::thread t2 = std::move(t1);   // Transfer ownership of the thread
t2.join();
```

In this example, ownership of the thread is transferred from t1 to t2 using std::move. After the move, t1 no longer represents a valid thread, and t2 is responsible for joining the thread.

Common Pitfalls in Multithreading

Multithreading offers significant performance benefits, but it also introduces complexity. Writing correct and efficient multithreaded code requires careful consideration of synchronization, resource management, and thread safety. In this section, we will explore some common pitfalls in multithreading and how to avoid them.

1. Race Conditions

A **race condition** occurs when multiple threads access a shared resource concurrently, and the outcome depends on the order in which the threads execute. Race conditions can lead to unpredictable behavior and are notoriously difficult to debug.

Example of a Race Condition:

```cpp
Copy code
#include <iostream>
#include <thread>

int counter = 0;

void incrementCounter() {
    for (int i = 0; i < 1000; ++i) {
```

```
        ++counter;
    }
}

int main() {
    std::thread t1(incrementCounter);
    std::thread t2(incrementCounter);

    t1.join();
    t2.join();

    std::cout << "Final counter value: " << counter << std::endl;
    return 0;
}
```

In this example, two threads (t1 and t2) increment the shared counter variable. Since both threads are modifying the same variable without proper synchronization, a race condition occurs. The final value of counter is unpredictable because the threads may interleave in different ways during execution.

Solution: Mutexes

To prevent race conditions, you need to ensure that only one thread accesses the shared resource at a time. This can be done using a **mutex** (std::mutex), which provides a way to lock the resource so that other threads must wait until the lock is released.

Example with Mutex:

```cpp
Copy code
#include <iostream>
#include <thread>
#include <mutex>

int counter = 0;
std::mutex mtx;
```

```cpp
void incrementCounter() {
    for (int i = 0; i < 1000; ++i) {
        std::lock_guard<std::mutex> lock(mtx);
        ++counter;
    }
}

int main() {
    std::thread t1(incrementCounter);
    std::thread t2(incrementCounter);

    t1.join();
    t2.join();

    std::cout << "Final counter value: " << counter << std::endl;
    return 0;
}
```

In this example, we use a std::mutex to synchronize access to the counter variable. The std::lock_guard automatically locks the mutex when it is created and releases the lock when it goes out of scope. This ensures that only one thread can modify the counter at a time, preventing race conditions.

2. Deadlocks

A **deadlock** occurs when two or more threads are waiting for each other to release resources, causing all of them to block indefinitely. Deadlocks can arise when multiple threads need to acquire multiple locks, but the order in which they acquire the locks leads to a circular dependency.

Example of a Deadlock:

```cpp
cpp
Copy code
#include <iostream>
#include <thread>
#include <mutex>

std::mutex mtx1;
```

```cpp
std::mutex mtx2;

void thread1() {
    std::lock_guard<std::mutex> lock1(mtx1);
    std::lock_guard<std::mutex> lock2(mtx2);
    std::cout << "Thread 1 acquired both locks" << std::endl;
}

void thread2() {
    std::lock_guard<std::mutex> lock2(mtx2);
    std::lock_guard<std::mutex> lock1(mtx1);
    std::cout << "Thread 2 acquired both locks" << std::endl;
}

int main() {
    std::thread t1(thread1);
    std::thread t2(thread2);

    t1.join();
    t2.join();

    return 0;
}
```

In this example, thread1 acquires mtx1 first and then tries to acquire mtx2. At the same time, thread2 acquires mtx2 and then tries to acquire mtx1. Since both threads are holding one lock and waiting for the other, they enter a deadlock and cannot proceed.

Solution: Lock Ordering

To avoid deadlocks, you should acquire locks in a consistent order. One approach is to always acquire the locks in the same sequence in all threads. Alternatively, C++ provides the std::lock() function, which locks multiple mutexes simultaneously without causing deadlocks.

Example with std::lock():

```cpp
Copy code
#include <iostream>
#include <thread>
#include <mutex>

std::mutex mtx1;
std::mutex mtx2;

void thread1() {
    std::lock(mtx1, mtx2);   // Lock both mutexes
    std::lock_guard<std::mutex> lock1(mtx1, std::adopt_lock);
    std::lock_guard<std::mutex> lock2(mtx2, std::adopt_lock);
    std::cout << "Thread 1 acquired both locks" << std::endl;
}

void thread2() {
    std::lock(mtx1, mtx2);   // Lock both mutexes
    std::lock_guard<std::mutex> lock1(mtx1, std::adopt_lock);
    std::lock_guard<std::mutex> lock2(mtx2, std::adopt_lock);
    std::cout << "Thread 2 acquired both locks" << std::endl;
}

int main() {
    std::thread t1(thread1);
    std::thread t2(thread2);

    t1.join();
    t2.join();

    return 0;
}
```

By using std::lock(), both threads acquire the locks without risk of deadlock, since std::lock() ensures that all mutexes are locked simultaneously.

3. Excessive Context Switching

Excessive context switching occurs when the operating system frequently switches between threads. Context switching involves saving the state of one thread and restoring the state of another, which can be expensive in terms of

CPU cycles. If there are too many threads running, the overhead of context switching can negate the benefits of concurrency.

To minimize context switching, it's essential to:

- Limit the number of threads to match the available hardware resources (e.g., the number of CPU cores).
- Use thread pools to manage a fixed number of threads for performing tasks.
- Avoid creating and destroying threads repeatedly. Reuse threads where possible.

4. Resource Contention

When multiple threads compete for the same resource, such as a file, database connection, or shared memory, it can lead to resource contention. Resource contention can degrade performance and lead to bottlenecks, especially in systems with many threads.

To reduce resource contention:

- Use finer-grained locks to lock smaller portions of shared resources.
- Minimize the amount of time a thread holds a lock.
- Use lock-free data structures and algorithms where possible.

5. Memory Consistency Issues

Multithreaded programs must ensure that memory writes from one thread are visible to other threads. Without proper synchronization, memory consistency issues can arise, where one thread may see stale or inconsistent data.

To prevent memory consistency issues, use:

- **Atomic operations** (std::atomic) for simple shared variables.
- **Mutexes** and **condition variables** for complex data structures.

Conclusion

In this chapter, we explored the basics of concurrency in C++, focusing on the std::thread class, thread creation and management, the thread lifecycle, and common pitfalls in multithreading. By understanding how to create, join, and detach threads, as well as how to avoid common issues like race conditions, deadlocks, and excessive context switching, you can write efficient and robust multithreaded applications in C++.

As you continue your journey into C++ concurrency, keep these fundamental concepts in mind, and always aim to write code that is both correct and efficient. In the next chapter, we will delve deeper into synchronization mechanisms, exploring mutexes, locks, and condition variables in detail.

Chapter 3: Synchronization in C++

In multithreaded programming, synchronization is one of the most crucial topics. Without proper synchronization, programs can exhibit unpredictable behavior, leading to race conditions, deadlocks, and other subtle bugs that are often difficult to debug. In this chapter, we will dive deep into synchronization mechanisms in C++, focusing on solving concurrency-related problems, particularly those related to shared resources. We will explore concepts like race conditions, mutexes, std::lock_guard, condition variables, deadlock avoidance, and the use of std::unique_lock and other locking mechanisms.

The Problem of Race Conditions

A **race condition** occurs when two or more threads access shared data simultaneously, and the outcome of the program depends on the timing of that access. Race conditions are among the most common and insidious problems in multithreaded programs. They typically arise when multiple threads read and write to a shared variable without proper synchronization.

Understanding Race Conditions

In a multithreaded program, a race condition can happen when:

1. Two or more threads access a shared resource (e.g., a variable or data structure).

2. At least one thread is writing to the shared resource.
3. The access to the shared resource is unsynchronized (i.e., no locking or synchronization is in place).

Let's look at an example to illustrate this problem.
Example of a Race Condition:

```cpp
Copy code
#include <iostream>
#include <thread>

int counter = 0;

void incrementCounter() {
    for (int i = 0; i < 100000; ++i) {
        ++counter;
    }
}

int main() {
    std::thread t1(incrementCounter);
    std::thread t2(incrementCounter);

    t1.join();
    t2.join();

    std::cout << "Final counter value: " << counter << std::endl;
    return 0;
}
```

In this example, both t1 and t2 threads are incrementing the counter variable. Since no synchronization is in place, both threads can access the shared counter variable simultaneously, causing a race condition. The final output of the program will likely be incorrect because the operations on the counter are not atomic (i.e., the increments are split into multiple steps such as reading, incrementing, and writing back the value).

A race condition occurs because both threads might read the same value of the counter before the increment and write the incremented value back, overwriting the other thread's update. As a result, the counter will not be incremented correctly.

Identifying and Fixing Race Conditions

Race conditions are typically challenging to detect and reproduce, as they depend on the exact timing of the thread execution. However, you can identify race conditions by looking for shared resources that are accessed by multiple threads and ensuring that access to those resources is synchronized.

To fix race conditions, we use synchronization primitives such as **mutexes** and **locks** to ensure that only one thread can access the shared resource at a time.

Mutexes: Locks and std::lock_guard

A **mutex** (short for "mutual exclusion") is a synchronization primitive that allows only one thread to access a shared resource at a time. When a thread locks a mutex, other threads attempting to lock the same mutex will block (wait) until the mutex is unlocked. This ensures that only one thread can access the critical section of code that manipulates the shared resource, preventing race conditions.

Basic Mutex Usage

The C++ Standard Library provides the std::mutex class for managing mutexes. A typical use case involves creating a mutex, locking it before accessing the shared resource, and unlocking it after the critical section has completed.

Example of Mutex Usage:

```
cpp
Copy code
#include <iostream>
#include <thread>
#include <mutex>
```

```cpp
int counter = 0;
std::mutex mtx;   // Create a mutex

void incrementCounter() {
    for (int i = 0; i < 100000; ++i) {
        mtx.lock();   // Lock the mutex before accessing the shared
        resource
        ++counter;
        mtx.unlock();   // Unlock the mutex after accessing the
        shared resource
    }
}

int main() {
    std::thread t1(incrementCounter);
    std::thread t2(incrementCounter);

    t1.join();
    t2.join();

    std::cout << "Final counter value: " << counter << std::endl;
    return 0;
}
```

In this example, the mtx.lock() call ensures that only one thread can access the counter at a time. Once a thread locks the mutex, other threads attempting to lock it will block until the first thread unlocks it with mtx.unlock().

This prevents the race condition we saw in the previous example by ensuring that the increment operation on counter is atomic—only one thread can perform it at a time.

Using std::lock_guard for RAII-Style Mutex Management

In C++, managing mutexes manually with lock() and unlock() can lead to problems, particularly if an exception is thrown within the critical section of code. If a thread forgets to unlock the mutex, it can cause a deadlock, where other threads are blocked indefinitely.

To prevent this, C++ provides the std::lock_guard class, which automatically locks a mutex when it is created and unlocks it when it goes out of scope.

This follows the RAII (Resource Acquisition Is Initialization) idiom, ensuring that the mutex is always properly unlocked, even in the event of an exception.

Example with std::lock_guard:

```cpp
Copy code
#include <iostream>
#include <thread>
#include <mutex>

int counter = 0;
std::mutex mtx;

void incrementCounter() {
    for (int i = 0; i < 100000; ++i) {
        std::lock_guard<std::mutex> lock(mtx);  // Lock the mutex using lock_guard
        ++counter;  // The mutex is automatically unlocked when lock goes out of scope
    }
}

int main() {
    std::thread t1(incrementCounter);
    std::thread t2(incrementCounter);

    t1.join();
    t2.join();

    std::cout << "Final counter value: " << counter << std::endl;
    return 0;
}
```

In this example, the std::lock_guard ensures that the mutex is properly unlocked when the lock_guard object goes out of scope (i.e., when the current iteration of the loop ends). This simplifies mutex management and reduces the chances of introducing errors like forgetting to unlock the mutex.

Performance Considerations with Mutexes

While mutexes solve race conditions, they also introduce some overhead.

Locking and unlocking a mutex involves system calls, which can be expensive. Additionally, if multiple threads frequently contend for the same mutex, the program may suffer from reduced performance due to threads blocking while waiting for the mutex to be available.

To minimize the performance impact of mutexes:

1. **Minimize the scope of critical sections**: Only lock the mutex for the shortest time possible.
2. **Use finer-grained locks**: Instead of using a single mutex to protect a large shared resource, consider using multiple mutexes to protect smaller parts of the resource.
3. **Avoid unnecessary locking**: If a shared resource is read-only, use std::shared_mutex or atomic operations instead of a full mutex.

Using Condition Variables for Synchronization

In addition to mutexes, another important synchronization mechanism in C++ is the **condition variable**. A condition variable allows threads to wait for a certain condition to become true before proceeding. Condition variables are typically used in conjunction with mutexes to allow one thread to signal another thread that a condition has been met.

The Concept of Condition Variables

A condition variable allows a thread to "sleep" until another thread signals that a condition has been met. This is useful in scenarios where one thread needs to wait for another thread to complete a task before it can proceed. For example, in a producer-consumer scenario, the consumer thread needs to wait for the producer to produce data before it can consume the data.

C++ provides the std::condition_variable class for working with condition variables. The basic operations are:

- wait(): Causes the current thread to block until another thread signals the condition variable.
- notify_one(): Wakes up one thread waiting on the condition variable.

- notify_all(): Wakes up all threads waiting on the condition variable.

Example: Producer-Consumer with Condition Variables

Let's implement a simple producer-consumer example using condition variables. The producer thread generates data, and the consumer thread processes the data. The consumer must wait for the producer to produce data before proceeding.

Example:

```cpp
Copy code
#include <iostream>
#include <thread>
#include <mutex>
#include <condition_variable>
#include <queue>

std::queue<int> dataQueue;
std::mutex mtx;
std::condition_variable cv;
bool done = false;

void producer() {
    for (int i = 1; i <= 5; ++i) {
        std::unique_lock<std::mutex> lock(mtx);
        dataQueue.push(i);
        std::cout << "Produced: " << i << std::endl;
        cv.notify_one();  // Notify the consumer that data is
        available
    }

    std::unique_lock<std::mutex> lock(mtx);
    done = true;
    cv.notify_one();  // Notify the consumer that no more data
    will be produced
}

void consumer() {
```

```
    while (true) {
        std::unique_lock<std::mutex> lock(mtx);
        cv.wait(lock, [] { return !dataQueue.empty() || done; });

        while (!dataQueue.empty()) {
            int value = dataQueue.front();
            dataQueue.pop();
            std::cout << "Consumed: " << value << std::endl;
        }

        if (done) break;
    }
}

int main() {
    std::thread prod(producer);
    std::thread cons(consumer);

    prod.join();
    cons.join();

    return 0;
}
```

In this example:

- The producer thread generates five pieces of data and adds them to dataQueue.
- The consumer thread waits for data to be available in the queue using the cv.wait() call.
- Once data is available, the consumer processes it and prints it out.
- The done flag is used to signal the consumer that the producer has finished producing data.

The cv.wait() call releases the mutex and puts the consumer thread to sleep until the condition variable is signaled by the producer thread using cv.notify_one().

Deadlock Avoidance Strategies

A **deadlock** occurs when two or more threads are blocked, each waiting for the other to release a resource. Deadlocks can cause programs to hang indefinitely and are one of the most challenging issues to debug in multithreaded programming.

Causes of Deadlocks

Deadlocks typically occur in the following situation:

1. **Mutual exclusion**: At least one thread holds a resource in non-shareable mode (e.g., a mutex).
2. **Hold and wait**: A thread holding at least one resource is waiting to acquire additional resources held by other threads.
3. **No preemption**: Resources cannot be forcibly taken away from a thread once they have been acquired.
4. **Circular wait**: Two or more threads form a cycle, where each thread waits for a resource held by another thread in the cycle.

For example, consider the following scenario:

- Thread A locks mutex1 and waits for mutex2.
- Thread B locks mutex2 and waits for mutex1.

Both threads are waiting for each other, leading to a deadlock.

Strategies for Avoiding Deadlocks

Several strategies can help you avoid deadlocks in multithreaded programs:

1. **Lock Ordering**

- Ensure that all threads acquire locks in the same order. This prevents circular wait conditions, which are the primary cause of deadlocks.
- For example, if thread A locks mutex1 first and then mutex2, all other threads should follow the same order to prevent deadlocks.

CHAPTER 3: SYNCHRONIZATION IN C++

1. **Using std::lock()**

- C++ provides the std::lock() function, which can lock multiple mutexes simultaneously. This eliminates the risk of deadlock by ensuring that all mutexes are locked in one atomic operation.
- Example:

```cpp
Copy code
std::lock(mtx1, mtx2);   // Lock both mutexes atomically
```

1. **Avoid Nested Locks**

- Avoid situations where one thread holds a lock and then tries to acquire another lock. This reduces the risk of deadlock by minimizing the number of resources a thread holds at any given time.

1. **Try-Lock Mechanism**

- Use the try_lock() function to attempt to acquire a lock without blocking. If the lock is not available, the thread can proceed with other work instead of waiting indefinitely.
- Example:

```cpp
Copy code
if (mtx.try_lock()) {
    // Perform work
    mtx.unlock();
} else {
```

```
    // Do other work
}
```

1. **Timeouts**

- Use timeouts with condition variables or locks to prevent threads from waiting indefinitely. If a thread cannot acquire a lock within a specified timeout period, it can release the resources it holds and try again later.

The Use of std::unique_lock and Locking Mechanisms

The C++ Standard Library provides several mechanisms for managing locks efficiently. One of the most versatile locking mechanisms is the std::unique_lock, which provides more flexibility than std::lock_guard.

std::unique_lock vs. std::lock_guard

While std::lock_guard automatically locks and unlocks a mutex in its constructor and destructor, std::unique_lock offers additional control over locking and unlocking.

The key features of std::unique_lock are:

- **Deferred Locking**: std::unique_lock allows you to create the lock object without immediately locking the mutex. You can lock the mutex at a later point using the lock() method.
- **Manual Unlocking**: You can unlock the mutex manually before the lock object goes out of scope using the unlock() method.
- **Ownership Transfer**: std::unique_lock supports transferring ownership of the lock to another std::unique_lock object using move semantics.

Example of std::unique_lock:

CHAPTER 3: SYNCHRONIZATION IN C++

```cpp
Copy code
#include <iostream>
#include <thread>
#include <mutex>

std::mutex mtx;

void task() {
    std::unique_lock<std::mutex> lock(mtx, std::defer_lock);  // Deferred locking
    // Perform some non-critical work here

    lock.lock();    // Lock the mutex when needed
    std::cout << "Task is running" << std::endl;
    lock.unlock();  // Manually unlock the mutex

    // Perform other work
    lock.lock();    // Lock the mutex again if necessary
    std::cout << "Task is finishing" << std::endl;
}

int main() {
    std::thread t1(task);
    std::thread t2(task);

    t1.join();
    t2.join();

    return 0;
}
```

In this example, std::unique_lock is used with deferred locking, allowing the thread to perform non-critical work before locking the mutex. This flexibility can improve performance and reduce the time the mutex is held.

Scoped Locking with std::scoped_lock

In C++17, the std::scoped_lock class was introduced as a simpler and more efficient way to lock multiple mutexes simultaneously. It provides a straightforward way to lock several mutexes without risking deadlocks.

Example of std::scoped_lock:

```cpp
Copy code
#include <iostream>
#include <thread>
#include <mutex>

std::mutex mtx1, mtx2;

void task() {
    std::scoped_lock lock(mtx1, mtx2);   // Lock both mutexes
    std::cout << "Task is running" << std::endl;
}

int main() {
    std::thread t1(task);
    std::thread t2(task);

    t1.join();
    t2.join();

    return 0;
}
```

In this example, std::scoped_lock ensures that both mtx1 and mtx2 are locked without risking deadlock. The scoped_lock object automatically unlocks both mutexes when it goes out of scope.

Conclusion

In this chapter, we explored the critical topic of synchronization in C++ and its role in ensuring safe and efficient multithreaded programs. We covered race conditions and how to fix them using mutexes and locks, including the RAII-style std::lock_guard and the more flexible std::unique_lock. We also discussed the importance of condition variables in scenarios like producer-consumer patterns, where threads need to synchronize their behavior.

Additionally, we examined common pitfalls like deadlocks and how to avoid them using strategies like lock ordering, std::lock(), and try_lock().

By mastering these synchronization techniques, you can build robust, multithreaded C++ applications that take full advantage of modern multicore systems while avoiding common concurrency problems. In the next chapter, we will dive into **asynchronous programming** and explore how it differs from traditional multithreading, offering new ways to build scalable and responsive applications.

Chapter 4: Thread Synchronization Mechanisms in C++

1. Introduction to Thread Synchronization

Thread synchronization is a crucial aspect of concurrent programming. It refers to the coordination of simultaneous threads to ensure that shared resources are accessed in a controlled manner. This chapter explores the various synchronization mechanisms available in C++, including mutexes, condition variables, atomic operations, and more.

1.1 Importance of Synchronization

With the rise of multicore processors and multithreading, synchronization becomes necessary to prevent data races and ensure data integrity. When multiple threads operate on shared data, synchronization mechanisms control access to this data, ensuring that only one thread can manipulate the data at a time, which is critical for maintaining consistency.

2. Mutexes and Locks

Mutexes (mutual exclusion locks) are one of the fundamental synchronization primitives in C++. They provide a way for threads to lock a resource so that only one thread can access it at any given time.

2.1 Basic Mutex Operations

Mutexes are straightforward to use in C++. To use a mutex:

- Create a mutex object.
- Lock the mutex before accessing the shared resource.
- Unlock the mutex after you are done with the resource.

Example:

```cpp
Copy code
#include <iostream>
#include <thread>
#include <mutex>

std::mutex mtx;

void printMessage(const std::string& message) {
    mtx.lock();    // Lock the mutex
    std::cout << message << std::endl;
    mtx.unlock();  // Unlock the mutex
}

int main() {
    std::thread t1(printMessage, "Hello from Thread 1");
    std::thread t2(printMessage, "Hello from Thread 2");

    t1.join();
    t2.join();

    return 0;
}
```

In this example, the mtx mutex ensures that the output from each thread is printed without interference.

2.2 Using std::lock_guard

While using mutexes directly with lock() and unlock() works, it can lead to errors if an exception occurs, preventing the mutex from being unlocked properly. To avoid this issue, you can use std::lock_guard, which automatically locks a mutex when it is created and unlocks it when it goes out of scope.

Example:

```cpp
Copy code
#include <iostream>
#include <thread>
#include <mutex>

std::mutex mtx;

void printMessage(const std::string& message) {
    std::lock_guard<std::mutex> lock(mtx);  // Lock the mutex
    std::cout << message << std::endl;  // Automatically unlocked
    when going out of scope
}

int main() {
    std::thread t1(printMessage, "Hello from Thread 1");
    std::thread t2(printMessage, "Hello from Thread 2");

    t1.join();
    t2.join();

    return 0;
}
```

3. Condition Variables

Condition variables are another essential synchronization primitive in C++. They allow threads to wait for certain conditions to occur before proceeding. Condition variables work in conjunction with mutexes to notify one or more waiting threads when a condition changes.

3.1 Using Condition Variables

The typical use case for condition variables is in producer-consumer

CHAPTER 4: THREAD SYNCHRONIZATION MECHANISMS IN C++

scenarios, where one thread (the producer) produces data and another thread (the consumer) consumes that data.

Example of Producer-Consumer:

```cpp
Copy code
#include <iostream>
#include <thread>
#include <mutex>
#include <condition_variable>
#include <queue>

std::queue<int> dataQueue;
std::mutex mtx;
std::condition_variable cv;
bool done = false;

void producer() {
    for (int i = 1; i <= 5; ++i) {
        std::lock_guard<std::mutex> lock(mtx);
        dataQueue.push(i);
        std::cout << "Produced: " << i << std::endl;
        cv.notify_one();   // Notify the consumer
    }
    std::lock_guard<std::mutex> lock(mtx);
    done = true;
    cv.notify_one();   // Notify the consumer that production is
    done
}

void consumer() {
    while (true) {
        std::unique_lock<std::mutex> lock(mtx);
        cv.wait(lock, [] { return !dataQueue.empty() || done; });

        while (!dataQueue.empty()) {
            int value = dataQueue.front();
            dataQueue.pop();
            std::cout << "Consumed: " << value << std::endl;
```

```
        }
        if (done) break;
    }
}

int main() {
    std::thread prodThread(producer);
    std::thread consThread(consumer);

    prodThread.join();
    consThread.join();

    return 0;
}
```

In this example, the producer adds items to the dataQueue, and the consumer waits for items to become available. The cv.wait() method releases the lock and blocks the thread until notified. When the producer adds an item, it calls cv.notify_one() to wake up the consumer.

3.2 Best Practices for Condition Variables

- Always use condition variables in conjunction with a mutex.
- Use a predicate to avoid spurious wakeups, ensuring that the condition is checked before proceeding.
- Notify waiting threads appropriately using notify_one() or notify_all() depending on your needs.

4. Atomic Operations

Atomic operations allow multiple threads to work with shared data without needing to lock mutexes explicitly. Atomic types in C++ guarantee that operations on these types are indivisible, preventing race conditions.

4.1 Using Atomic Types

C++ provides the std::atomic template to define atomic types. These types include basic types like integers and booleans.

CHAPTER 4: THREAD SYNCHRONIZATION MECHANISMS IN C++

Example:

```cpp
Copy code
#include <iostream>
#include <thread>
#include <atomic>

std::atomic<int> counter(0);  // Atomic counter

void incrementCounter() {
    for (int i = 0; i < 1000; ++i) {
        ++counter;  // Atomic increment
    }
}

int main() {
    std::thread t1(incrementCounter);
    std::thread t2(incrementCounter);

    t1.join();
    t2.join();

    std::cout << "Final counter value: " << counter << std::endl;

    return 0;
}
```

In this example, the counter variable is defined as an atomic integer. The ++counter operation is guaranteed to be atomic, so it can be safely used by multiple threads without additional synchronization.

4.2 Benefits of Atomic Operations

- **Performance**: Atomic operations are typically faster than using mutexes since they do not involve locking overhead.
- **Simplicity**: Using atomic operations reduces the complexity of the code by eliminating the need for explicit locking mechanisms.

5. Advanced Locking Mechanisms

In addition to basic mutexes and condition variables, C++ offers several advanced locking mechanisms that provide more flexibility and control over synchronization.

5.1 std::unique_lock

The std::unique_lock class provides more control than std::lock_guard. It allows you to lock and unlock a mutex manually and supports deferred locking.

Example:

```cpp
Copy code
#include <iostream>
#include <thread>
#include <mutex>

std::mutex mtx;

void criticalSection() {
    std::unique_lock<std::mutex> lock(mtx);
    std::cout << "In critical section" << std::endl;
    // Lock will be released when unique_lock goes out of scope
}

int main() {
    std::thread t1(criticalSection);
    std::thread t2(criticalSection);

    t1.join();
    t2.join();

    return 0;
}
```

In this example, std::unique_lock manages the locking of the mutex, ensuring it is unlocked when the lock object goes out of scope.

5.2 Shared Mutexes

CHAPTER 4: THREAD SYNCHRONIZATION MECHANISMS IN C++

C++ also provides **shared mutexes** (std::shared_mutex), which allow multiple threads to read shared data simultaneously while providing exclusive access for write operations.

Example of Shared Mutex:

```cpp
Copy code
#include <iostream>
#include <thread>
#include <shared_mutex>
#include <vector>

std::shared_mutex sharedMtx;
std::vector<int> sharedData;

void readData() {
    std::shared_lock<std::shared_mutex> lock(sharedMtx);  // Shared lock for reading
    for (const auto& value : sharedData) {
        std::cout << "Reading: " << value << std::endl;
    }
}

void writeData(int value) {
    std::unique_lock<std::shared_mutex> lock(sharedMtx);  // Exclusive lock for writing
    sharedData.push_back(value);
    std::cout << "Writing: " << value << std::endl;
}

int main() {
    std::thread t1(writeData, 10);
    std::thread t2(readData);
    std::thread t3(writeData, 20);
    std::thread t4(readData);

    t1.join();
    t2.join();
    t3.join();
```

```
    t4.join();

    return 0;
}
```

In this example, multiple threads can read from sharedData simultaneously using std::shared_lock, while exclusive write access is managed with std::unique_lock. This improves performance when read operations are frequent.

5.3 Spinlocks

Spinlocks are another locking mechanism that provides a lightweight alternative to traditional mutexes. When a thread attempts to acquire a spinlock and the lock is already held by another thread, the thread will "spin" in a loop, repeatedly checking the lock until it becomes available. While spinlocks can be efficient for short waits, they can lead to high CPU usage if the wait is prolonged.

Example of Spinlock:

```cpp
Copy code
#include <iostream>
#include <atomic>
#include <thread>

class Spinlock {
public:
    void lock() {
        while (flag.test_and_set(std::memory_order_acquire)) {
            // Spin wait (do nothing)
        }
    }

    void unlock() {
        flag.clear(std::memory_order_release);
    }
```

```cpp
private:
    std::atomic_flag flag = ATOMIC_FLAG_INIT;  // Atomic flag for
    the spinlock
};

Spinlock spinlock;
int sharedCounter = 0;

void increment() {
    for (int i = 0; i < 1000; ++i) {
        spinlock.lock();
        ++sharedCounter;
        spinlock.unlock();
    }
}

int main() {
    std::thread t1(increment);
    std::thread t2(increment);

    t1.join();
    t2.join();

    std::cout << "Final counter value: " << sharedCounter <<
    std::endl;

    return 0;
}
```

In this example, the Spinlock class uses an std::atomic_flag to manage locking. The thread will continue to check the lock until it can acquire it.

6. Summary

In this chapter, we delved into various synchronization mechanisms in C++. We started with the fundamental problem of race conditions, explored mutexes and locks, and introduced condition variables for managing thread synchronization. We also examined atomic operations as a lightweight alternative for synchronization and discussed advanced locking mechanisms such as std::unique_lock, shared mutexes, and spinlocks.

Understanding these synchronization mechanisms is essential for writing correct and efficient multithreaded applications. Proper synchronization allows you to control access to shared resources, prevent race conditions, and ensure data integrity. As you continue your journey into C++ concurrency, mastering these synchronization techniques will enable you to build robust, high-performance applications.

In the next chapter, we will explore **asynchronous programming** in C++, discussing how it differs from traditional multithreading and how to utilize C++'s asynchronous capabilities to create scalable and responsive applications.

Chapter 5: Advanced Thread Management in C++

As we delve deeper into the world of multithreading with C++, it's essential to understand advanced thread management techniques. In this chapter, we will explore various advanced topics, including thread pools, the std::async mechanism for asynchronous programming, handling exceptions in threads, and performance considerations when working with threads. Mastery of these concepts will enhance your ability to write efficient, scalable, and maintainable multithreaded applications.

1. Introduction to Advanced Thread Management

In modern applications, managing threads effectively is critical for performance and responsiveness. As we've seen in previous chapters, basic threading constructs like std::thread and synchronization mechanisms like mutexes and condition variables form the foundation of multithreading in C++. However, for complex applications, we need to leverage advanced techniques to efficiently manage thread lifecycles, optimize resource usage, and simplify concurrency.

1.1 Overview of Thread Management

Effective thread management involves:

- **Creating and destroying threads efficiently**: Avoiding the overhead of frequently creating and destroying threads by using thread pools.
- **Scheduling tasks**: Distributing work across threads to ensure that all CPU cores are utilized effectively.
- **Managing the lifecycle of threads**: Handling thread completion and exceptions gracefully.
- **Improving performance**: Identifying bottlenecks and optimizing thread usage.

2. Thread Pools

A **thread pool** is a collection of pre-instantiated threads that can be reused for executing tasks. Instead of creating a new thread for each task, a thread pool allows you to manage a fixed number of threads that can be assigned to multiple tasks. This approach reduces the overhead associated with thread creation and destruction and helps manage system resources more effectively.

2.1 Benefits of Using Thread Pools

- **Reduced Overhead**: Creating and destroying threads can be expensive in terms of CPU cycles. Thread pools eliminate this overhead by reusing existing threads.
- **Controlled Resource Usage**: By limiting the number of threads in the pool, you can prevent excessive resource consumption, avoiding scenarios where too many threads compete for CPU time.
- **Improved Performance**: Thread pools can improve the overall responsiveness and throughput of applications by efficiently managing task execution.

2.2 Implementing a Simple Thread Pool

Let's look at a basic implementation of a thread pool in C++. This example will create a fixed number of worker threads that can execute tasks queued by the main thread.

Example: Simple Thread Pool Implementation

CHAPTER 5: ADVANCED THREAD MANAGEMENT IN C++

```cpp
Copy code
#include <iostream>
#include <thread>
#include <vector>
#include <queue>
#include <functional>
#include <condition_variable>
#include <atomic>

class ThreadPool {
public:
    ThreadPool(size_t numThreads);
    ~ThreadPool();

    void enqueue(std::function<void()> task);

private:
    std::vector<std::thread> workers;
    std::queue<std::function<void()>> tasks;

    std::mutex mtx;
    std::condition_variable condition;
    std::atomic<bool> stop;

    void worker();
};

ThreadPool::ThreadPool(size_t numThreads) : stop(false) {
    for (size_t i = 0; i < numThreads; ++i) {
        workers.emplace_back([this] { this->worker(); });
    }
}

ThreadPool::~ThreadPool() {
    stop = true;
    condition.notify_all();   // Wake up all threads
    for (std::thread &worker : workers) {
```

```cpp
        worker.join();  // Wait for all threads to finish
    }
}

void ThreadPool::enqueue(std::function<void()> task) {
    {
        std::lock_guard<std::mutex> lock(mtx);
        tasks.push(std::move(task));
    }
    condition.notify_one();  // Notify one waiting thread
}

void ThreadPool::worker() {
    while (true) {
        std::function<void()> task;

        {
            std::unique_lock<std::mutex> lock(mtx);
            condition.wait(lock, [this] { return stop ||
            !tasks.empty(); });
            if (stop && tasks.empty()) return;  // Exit if stopping
            task = std::move(tasks.front());
            tasks.pop();
        }

        task();  // Execute the task
    }
}

void printMessage(int id) {
    std::cout << "Task " << id << " is being processed." <<
    std::endl;
}

int main() {
    ThreadPool pool(4);  // Create a thread pool with 4 threads

    // Enqueue tasks
    for (int i = 0; i < 10; ++i) {
        pool.enqueue([i] { printMessage(i); });
```

```
    }

    // Destructor of ThreadPool will wait for all tasks to finish
    return 0;
}
```

In this implementation:

- The ThreadPool class manages a vector of worker threads and a queue of tasks.
- The enqueue method adds tasks to the queue and notifies one waiting thread.
- Each worker runs in a loop, waiting for tasks to be enqueued and executing them.

2.3 Advanced Thread Pool Features

While the basic thread pool implementation is useful, it can be enhanced with additional features such as:

- **Dynamic Resizing**: Allowing the pool to grow or shrink based on the workload.
- **Task Prioritization**: Implementing priority queues to ensure critical tasks are executed first.
- **Error Handling**: Providing mechanisms for handling exceptions that occur during task execution.

3. Asynchronous Programming with std::async

In C++, the std::async function provides a simple way to execute functions asynchronously. It allows you to run a function in a separate thread and obtain its result in the future. This simplifies concurrent programming by abstracting away the thread management details.

3.1 Overview of std::async

The std::async function launches a function asynchronously, returning a std::future object that represents the eventual result of the function. This allows you to obtain the result of the asynchronous operation without blocking the main thread.

Example: Using std::async

```cpp
Copy code
#include <iostream>
#include <future>
#include <thread>

int compute(int value) {
    std::this_thread::sleep_for(std::chrono::seconds(2)); // Simulate long computation
    return value * 2;
}

int main() {
    std::future<int> result = std::async(std::launch::async, compute, 10);

    // Do other work while compute is running
    std::cout << "Doing other work..." << std::endl;

    // Get the result from the future (blocks if the computation is not finished)
    std::cout << "Result: " << result.get() << std::endl;

    return 0;
}
```

In this example, the compute function runs asynchronously, and the main thread can continue executing other tasks. When the result is needed, result.get() is called, which blocks until the computation is complete.

3.2 Launch Policies with std::async

The std::async function takes a launch policy as its first argument, which controls how the function is executed:

CHAPTER 5: ADVANCED THREAD MANAGEMENT IN C++

- std::launch::async: The function is executed in a new thread.
- std::launch::deferred: The function is executed lazily, meaning it will not run until get() is called. In this case, the computation will happen in the same thread that calls get().
- By default, the implementation may choose either policy.

Example of Launch Policies:

```cpp
Copy code
#include <iostream>
#include <future>
#include <thread>

void deferredTask() {
    std::cout << "Deferred task executed!" << std::endl;
}

int main() {
    std::future<void> result = std::async(std::launch::deferred, deferredTask);

    std::cout << "Doing other work..." << std::endl;

    // The deferred task runs only when get() is called
    result.get();

    return 0;
}
```

In this example, the deferredTask function is executed only when result.get() is called. The main thread can continue doing other work, and the deferred task will not block it.

4. Handling Exceptions in Threads

When dealing with multithreading, exceptions can occur for various reasons, such as accessing invalid memory, failing to allocate resources, or logic errors. Handling exceptions properly in a multithreaded environment is crucial for maintaining application stability.

4.1 Propagating Exceptions from Threads

When an exception occurs in a thread, it does not propagate automatically to the calling thread. Instead, it can be captured using std::future. If a thread function throws an exception, that exception can be retrieved from the future when calling get().

Example of Exception Handling in Threads:

```cpp
Copy code
#include <iostream>
#include <thread>
#include <future>
#include <stdexcept>

int mightThrow(int value) {
    if (value < 0) {
        throw std::invalid_argument("Negative value not allowed");
    }
    return value * 2;
}

int main() {
    std::future<int> result = std::async(std::launch::async,
    mightThrow, -10);

    try {
        // Attempt to get the result, which may throw an exception
        std::cout << "Result: " << result.get() << std::endl;
    } catch (const std::exception& e) {
        std::cout << "Exception caught: " << e.what() << std::endl;
    }
```

```
    return 0;
}
```

In this example, calling mightThrow with a negative value throws an exception. When we call result.get(), it rethrows the exception, allowing us to catch it in the main thread.

4.2 Ensuring Thread Safety During Exception Handling

When handling exceptions in a multithreaded context, it is essential to ensure that shared resources are accessed safely. If an exception occurs, locks must be managed correctly to prevent resource leaks or deadlocks.

Using smart pointers or RAII-style locking (like std::lock_guard) can help manage resources safely even when exceptions occur.

5. Performance Considerations with Threads

Performance is a critical aspect of multithreaded applications. While threads can help improve responsiveness and throughput, improper use can lead to performance degradation. This section will cover key performance considerations to keep in mind when working with threads.

5.1 Thread Overhead

Creating and destroying threads can introduce significant overhead, particularly if threads are created and destroyed frequently. To minimize this overhead:

- Use thread pools to manage a fixed number of threads.
- Avoid creating and destroying threads within performance-critical loops.

5.2 Context Switching

When multiple threads compete for CPU time, the operating system performs **context switching** to allocate CPU resources to the active threads. Excessive context switching can degrade performance, leading to increased CPU usage and reduced throughput. To minimize context switching:

- Limit the number of active threads to the number of available CPU cores.
- Use thread pools to manage concurrent tasks efficiently.

5.3 Lock Contention

When multiple threads attempt to acquire the same lock simultaneously, it can lead to **lock contention**, where threads are blocked while waiting for a lock to become available. This can cause performance bottlenecks. To minimize lock contention:

- Use finer-grained locks to reduce the scope of locked sections.
- Consider using lock-free data structures and algorithms when appropriate.

5.4 Profiling and Optimization

To identify performance issues in multithreaded applications, use profiling tools to analyze thread behavior and resource usage. Profilers can help identify bottlenecks, excessive context switching, and lock contention.

6. Conclusion

In this chapter, we explored advanced thread management techniques in C++. We covered the importance of thread pools, the std::async function for asynchronous programming, and how to handle exceptions in threads. We also discussed performance considerations, including thread overhead, context switching, and lock contention.

Mastering these advanced techniques will enable you to write efficient, responsive, and scalable multithreaded applications in C++. In the next chapter, we will focus on **design patterns for concurrent programming**, providing you with strategies to structure your code effectively for multithreading.

Chapter 6: Designing Patterns for Concurrency in C++

Designing concurrent systems requires not just knowledge of synchronization and threading primitives, but also an understanding of how to structure your code effectively. This chapter focuses on various design patterns that can be employed in concurrent programming with C++. We will cover common concurrency patterns such as the Producer-Consumer, Reader-Writer, and Future patterns, as well as explore best practices for implementing these patterns. By the end of this chapter, you will have a toolkit of design patterns to help you build robust multithreaded applications.

1. Introduction to Concurrency Design Patterns

Concurrency design patterns provide solutions to common problems encountered when developing multithreaded applications. They offer a way to structure your code so that it is easier to understand, maintain, and extend. Design patterns in concurrency are essential for:

- **Simplifying code**: By using established patterns, you can write cleaner and more organized code that is easier to follow.
- **Improving performance**: Patterns can help you optimize resource

usage and avoid common pitfalls like race conditions and deadlocks.
- **Facilitating collaboration**: Design patterns provide a shared vocabulary for discussing and implementing concurrent systems.

2. The Producer-Consumer Pattern

The **Producer-Consumer** pattern is one of the most common concurrency patterns. It involves two types of threads: producers that generate data and consumers that process the data. The challenge is to synchronize access to a shared buffer where the data is stored.

2.1 Overview of the Producer-Consumer Pattern

- **Producers** add items to a shared buffer.
- **Consumers** remove items from the buffer and process them.
- The buffer can be implemented as a queue, and proper synchronization is required to prevent race conditions.

2.2 Implementing the Producer-Consumer Pattern in C++

Let's implement a simple Producer-Consumer example using C++ threads, mutexes, and condition variables.

Example: Producer-Consumer Implementation

```cpp
Copy code
#include <iostream>
#include <thread>
#include <mutex>
#include <condition_variable>
#include <queue>
#include <chrono>

std::queue<int> buffer;      // Shared buffer
std::mutex mtx;              // Mutex for synchronizing access to the buffer
std::condition_variable cv;  // Condition variable for signaling
```

```cpp
const int bufferSize = 5;    // Maximum size of the buffer
bool done = false;           // Flag to indicate when production
is finished

void producer() {
    for (int i = 1; i <= 10; ++i) {
        std::this_thread::sleep_for(std::chrono::milliseconds(100));
         // Simulate work
        std::unique_lock<std::mutex> lock(mtx);
        // Wait until there is space in the buffer
        cv.wait(lock, [] { return buffer.size() < bufferSize; });
        buffer.push(i);
        std::cout << "Produced: " << i << std::endl;
        lock.unlock();
        cv.notify_one();  // Notify a waiting consumer
    }
    done = true;
    cv.notify_all();  // Notify all consumers that production is
    done
}

void consumer() {
    while (true) {
        std::unique_lock<std::mutex> lock(mtx);
        // Wait until there is data in the buffer or production is
        done
        cv.wait(lock, [] { return !buffer.empty() || done; });
        if (buffer.empty() && done) break;  // Exit if done and
        buffer is empty
        if (!buffer.empty()) {
            int value = buffer.front();
            buffer.pop();
            std::cout << "Consumed: " << value << std::endl;
        }
        lock.unlock();
        cv.notify_one();  // Notify a waiting producer
    }
}

int main() {
```

```
    std::thread prodThread(producer);
    std::thread consThread(consumer);

    prodThread.join();
    consThread.join();

    return 0;
}
```

In this implementation:

- The producer thread generates numbers and adds them to the shared buffer.
- The consumer thread retrieves numbers from the buffer and processes them.
- A condition variable is used to notify consumers when data is available and producers when there is space in the buffer.

3. The Reader-Writer Pattern

The **Reader-Writer** pattern allows multiple threads to read shared data simultaneously while ensuring that write operations are exclusive. This pattern is useful in scenarios where read operations are frequent, and write operations are infrequent.

3.1 Overview of the Reader-Writer Pattern

- **Readers** can access the shared resource simultaneously.
- **Writers** require exclusive access to the shared resource.
- Proper synchronization is needed to prevent readers from accessing data while a writer is modifying it.

3.2 Implementing the Reader-Writer Pattern in C++

Let's implement a simple Reader-Writer example using C++ threads, mutexes, and condition variables.

CHAPTER 6: DESIGNING PATTERNS FOR CONCURRENCY IN C++

Example: Reader-Writer Implementation

```cpp
Copy code
#include <iostream>
#include <thread>
#include <mutex>
#include <shared_mutex>
#include <chrono>

std::shared_mutex rwMutex;   // Shared mutex for reader-writer access
int sharedData = 0;          // Shared resource

void reader(int id) {
    for (int i = 0; i < 3; ++i) {
        std::this_thread::sleep_for(std::chrono::milliseconds(100));
         // Simulate work
        std::shared_lock<std::shared_mutex> lock(rwMutex);  //
        Acquire shared lock
        std::cout << "Reader " << id << " read data: " <<
        sharedData << std::endl;
    }
}

void writer(int id) {
    for (int i = 0; i < 3; ++i) {
        std::this_thread::sleep_for(std::chrono::milliseconds(150));
         // Simulate work
        std::unique_lock<std::shared_mutex> lock(rwMutex);  //
        Acquire exclusive lock
        sharedData += 1;   // Modify shared resource
        std::cout << "Writer " << id << " wrote data: " <<
        sharedData << std::endl;
    }
}

int main() {
    std::thread r1(reader, 1);
    std::thread r2(reader, 2);
```

```
    std::thread w1(writer, 1);
    std::thread w2(writer, 2);

    r1.join();
    r2.join();
    w1.join();
    w2.join();

    return 0;
}
```

In this example:

- Multiple reader threads can read the sharedData simultaneously using a std::shared_lock.
- Writer threads modify sharedData using a std::unique_lock, ensuring that no readers can access it while it is being modified.

4. Future and Promise Patterns

The **Future and Promise** pattern is a way to represent a value that may not yet be available. This pattern is useful in asynchronous programming, where a computation might take some time to complete.

4.1 Overview of Futures and Promises

- A **promise** is a way to set a value or an exception at some point in the future.
- A **future** is a way to retrieve that value or exception when it becomes available.
- This pattern allows one thread to produce a value and another thread to consume it without blocking.

4.2 Using std::promise and std::future

Let's look at an example that demonstrates the use of std::promise and std::future.

Example: Future and Promise Implementation

```cpp
Copy code
#include <iostream>
#include <thread>
#include <future>
#include <chrono>

void compute(std::promise<int>& prom) {
    std::this_thread::sleep_for(std::chrono::seconds(2));  // Simulate computation
    prom.set_value(42);  // Set the computed value
}

int main() {
    std::promise<int> prom;  // Create a promise
    std::future<int> fut = prom.get_future();  // Get the future associated with the promise

    std::thread t(compute, std::ref(prom));  // Launch a thread to perform computation

    // Do other work while waiting for the future
    std::cout << "Waiting for result..." << std::endl;
    int result = fut.get();  // Wait for the result

    std::cout << "Result: " << result << std::endl;

    t.join();  // Wait for the computation thread to finish
    return 0;
}
```

In this example, a promise is created to hold the result of the computation. The compute function simulates a long-running computation and sets the computed value using the promise. The main thread retrieves the result using the future associated with the promise.

5. Fork-Join Pattern

The **Fork-Join** pattern is a common approach for parallelizing tasks. It involves splitting a task into smaller subtasks (forking) that can be processed in parallel, and then combining the results (joining) once the subtasks are completed.

5.1 Overview of the Fork-Join Pattern

1. **Forking**: The main task is divided into smaller subtasks, each of which can be executed concurrently.
2. **Joining**: After all subtasks are completed, the results are combined to produce the final output.

5.2 Implementing the Fork-Join Pattern in C++

Let's implement a simple Fork-Join example using C++ threads and futures.

Example: Fork-Join Implementation

```cpp
Copy code
#include <iostream>
#include <thread>
#include <future>
#include <vector>

int compute(int value) {
    return value * value;  // Simple computation
}

int main() {
    std::vector<int> values = {1, 2, 3, 4, 5};  // Input values
    std::vector<std::future<int>> futures;  // Store futures for results

    // Fork: Launch tasks to compute squares in parallel
    for (const auto& value : values) {
        futures.push_back(std::async(std::launch::async, compute,
```

```
        value));
    }
    
    // Join: Collect results
    for (auto& fut : futures) {
        std::cout << "Result: " << fut.get() << std::endl;
    }
    
    return 0;
}
```

In this example, the main task is to compute the squares of a list of values. Each computation is launched as an asynchronous task using std::async, and the results are collected after all tasks are completed.

6. Best Practices for Concurrent Programming

When designing and implementing concurrent systems, adhering to best practices can help you avoid common pitfalls and create robust applications. Here are some best practices to keep in mind:

6.1 Keep Critical Sections Short

Minimize the amount of code within critical sections (code that holds locks). This reduces the likelihood of contention and makes your application more responsive.

6.2 Use Appropriate Synchronization Mechanisms

Choose the right synchronization mechanism for the task at hand. Use mutexes for exclusive access, condition variables for signaling, and atomic operations for simple shared variables.

6.3 Prefer Lock-Free Structures When Possible

When applicable, consider using lock-free data structures and algorithms to reduce contention and improve performance. However, these can be complex and may not be suitable for all scenarios.

6.4 Document Threading Behavior

Document the threading behavior of your code. Clearly outline which parts of your code are thread-safe and which are not. This will help other developers (and your future self) understand how to use the code correctly.

6.5 Handle Exceptions Gracefully

Ensure that your threads can handle exceptions gracefully. Use std::future to propagate exceptions and handle them in the main thread.

6.6 Test for Concurrency Issues

Use testing frameworks and tools that can help identify concurrency issues such as race conditions and deadlocks. Consider stress testing your application under high load to observe its behavior.

7. Conclusion

In this chapter, we explored various design patterns for concurrency in C++. We covered the Producer-Consumer and Reader-Writer patterns, as well as the Future and Promise patterns. We also discussed the Fork-Join pattern for parallelizing tasks and explored best practices for writing robust multithreaded applications.

Mastering these concurrency design patterns will enable you to build scalable and efficient C++ applications that leverage the full power of modern multicore processors. In the next chapter, we will delve into **real-world applications** of C++ concurrency, showcasing how these concepts can be applied to solve practical problems in various domains.

Chapter 7: Real-World Applications of C++ Concurrency

In this chapter, we will explore how concurrency in C++ can be applied to solve real-world problems across various domains. We will cover several practical use cases, including web servers, game development, financial systems, scientific computing, and more. Each section will demonstrate how to utilize the concurrency concepts and design patterns discussed in previous chapters to create efficient, responsive applications. By understanding these applications, you will gain insights into the practical implementation of concurrency in C++.

1. Introduction to Real-World Applications

Concurrency is an essential aspect of modern software development, especially as applications become more complex and require higher performance. With the rise of multicore processors, the ability to manage multiple tasks simultaneously has become a critical factor in designing scalable applications. This chapter will showcase various real-world scenarios where concurrency can significantly enhance application performance and responsiveness.

1.1 Importance of Concurrency in Applications

- **Performance Improvement**: By leveraging concurrency, applications

can perform multiple tasks in parallel, leading to improved throughput and reduced latency.
- **Responsiveness**: Concurrency enables applications to remain responsive to user interactions while performing background processing.
- **Resource Utilization**: Efficiently utilizing available hardware resources is crucial for maximizing performance and efficiency.

2. Building a Multithreaded Web Server

Web servers handle multiple client requests simultaneously, making concurrency a fundamental aspect of their design. A multithreaded web server can manage connections from many clients concurrently, improving response times and overall performance.

2.1 Overview of Web Server Architecture

A simple multithreaded web server typically consists of the following components:

- **Listener**: A thread that listens for incoming client connections.
- **Worker Threads**: Threads that handle the processing of requests from clients.
- **Request Queue**: A shared queue to manage incoming requests.
- **Response Handling**: Mechanisms to send responses back to clients.

2.2 Implementing a Basic Multithreaded Web Server

Let's implement a simple multithreaded web server using C++. This server will listen for incoming HTTP requests and respond with a basic message.

Example: Multithreaded Web Server Implementation

```cpp
Copy code
#include <iostream>
#include <thread>
#include <mutex>
```

CHAPTER 7: REAL-WORLD APPLICATIONS OF C++ CONCURRENCY

```cpp
#include <vector>
#include <queue>
#include <cstring>
#include <arpa/inet.h>
#include <unistd.h>

const int PORT = 8080;
std::mutex mtx;  // Mutex for synchronizing access to shared resources

void handleRequest(int clientSocket) {
    char buffer[1024];
    std::memset(buffer, 0, sizeof(buffer));

    // Read the request from the client
    read(clientSocket, buffer, sizeof(buffer));
    std::cout << "Request received:\n" << buffer << std::endl;

    // Send a simple HTTP response
    const char* response = "HTTP/1.1 200 OK\r\nContent-Length: 13\r\n\r\nHello, World!";
    write(clientSocket, response, strlen(response));

    // Close the client socket
    close(clientSocket);
}

void serverLoop() {
    int serverSocket, clientSocket;
    struct sockaddr_in serverAddr, clientAddr;
    socklen_t clientAddrLen = sizeof(clientAddr);

    // Create socket
    serverSocket = socket(AF_INET, SOCK_STREAM, 0);
    serverAddr.sin_family = AF_INET;
    serverAddr.sin_addr.s_addr = INADDR_ANY;
    serverAddr.sin_port = htons(PORT);

    // Bind the socket
    bind(serverSocket, (struct sockaddr*)&serverAddr,
```

```
        sizeof(serverAddr));
    listen(serverSocket, 5);   // Listen for incoming connections

    std::cout << "Server is listening on port " << PORT <<
    std::endl;

    while (true) {
        // Accept a client connection
        clientSocket = accept(serverSocket, (struct
        sockaddr*)&clientAddr, &clientAddrLen);

        // Spawn a new thread to handle the client request
        std::thread(handleRequest, clientSocket).detach();    //
        Detach the thread to allow independent execution
    }

    close(serverSocket);
}

int main() {
    std::thread serverThread(serverLoop);
    serverThread.join();   // Wait for the server thread to finish
    return 0;
}
```

In this implementation:

- The server creates a listening socket and accepts incoming connections.
- Each client connection is handled in a separate thread using std::thread, allowing multiple clients to be served concurrently.
- The server responds with a simple HTTP message.

2.3 Enhancements for a Production-Ready Server

While this example demonstrates a basic multithreaded web server, several enhancements can be made for production readiness:

- **Connection Pooling**: Manage client connections efficiently by reusing

them.
- **Request Queue**: Implement a request queue for handling a large number of concurrent connections.
- **Logging and Error Handling**: Add logging mechanisms and error handling for robustness.
- **Security Features**: Implement HTTPS and input validation to enhance security.

3. Game Development and Concurrency

Game development is another domain where concurrency plays a critical role. Games often involve complex simulations and require smooth rendering, user input handling, and networking. Proper use of concurrency can significantly enhance the gaming experience.

3.1 Overview of Game Architecture

A typical game architecture may include:

- **Game Loop**: A main loop that continuously updates the game state and renders graphics.
- **Rendering Thread**: A dedicated thread for rendering graphics to ensure smooth visuals.
- **Input Handling**: A thread for processing user input (keyboard, mouse, etc.).
- **Physics Simulation**: A thread for handling physics calculations and collision detection.

3.2 Implementing a Simple Game Loop with Concurrency

Let's implement a basic game loop that utilizes concurrency for rendering and input handling.

Example: Basic Game Loop Implementation

```cpp
Copy code
#include <iostream>
#include <thread>
#include <atomic>
#include <chrono>

std::atomic<bool> running(true);  // Flag to control the game loop

void render() {
    while (running) {
        // Simulate rendering work
        std::this_thread::sleep_for(std::chrono::milliseconds(16));
         // Simulate frame time
        std::cout << "Rendering frame..." << std::endl;
    }
}

void handleInput() {
    char input;
    while (running) {
        std::cin >> input;  // Get user input
        if (input == 'q') {  // Quit command
            running = false;  // Stop the game loop
        }
    }
}

int main() {
    std::thread renderThread(render);  // Start the rendering thread
    std::thread inputThread(handleInput);  // Start the input handling thread

    renderThread.join();  // Wait for the rendering thread to finish
    inputThread.join();  // Wait for the input handling thread to finish

    std::cout << "Game has ended." << std::endl;
```

```
    return 0;
}
```

In this example:

- The render function simulates the rendering of frames in a game.
- The handleInput function listens for user input, allowing the player to quit the game.
- The game loop runs concurrently, enabling rendering and input handling to occur simultaneously.

3.3 Synchronization in Game Development

In a more complex game, you may have shared resources that require synchronization. For example, if multiple threads access shared game state (e.g., player position, game scores), you must use mutexes or other synchronization mechanisms to ensure thread safety.

4. Financial Systems and Concurrency

Financial systems, such as trading platforms and banking applications, often require high throughput and low latency. Concurrency is essential for handling multiple transactions, real-time data feeds, and ensuring data consistency.

4.1 Overview of Financial System Architecture

A financial system may consist of:

- **Order Processing**: Handling incoming trade orders from users.
- **Market Data Feeds**: Receiving and processing real-time market data.
- **Risk Management**: Evaluating risk for open positions.
- **Reporting**: Generating reports for transactions and account balances.

4.2 Implementing a Simple Order Processing System

Let's implement a basic order processing system using C++ concurrency.

Example: Simple Order Processing System

```cpp
Copy code
#include <iostream>
#include <thread>
#include <mutex>
#include <queue>
#include <chrono>

std::queue<int> orderQueue;    // Queue for incoming orders
std::mutex orderMutex;         // Mutex for synchronizing access to the order queue
bool done = false;             // Flag to indicate when processing is done

void processOrders() {
    while (!done || !orderQueue.empty()) {
        std::this_thread::sleep_for(std::chrono::milliseconds(100));
         // Simulate processing time

        std::unique_lock<std::mutex> lock(orderMutex);
        if (!orderQueue.empty()) {
            int order = orderQueue.front();
            orderQueue.pop();
            lock.unlock();  // Unlock before processing to allow others to access the queue

            std::cout << "Processing order: " << order << std::endl;
        }
    }
}

void generateOrders() {
    for (int i = 1; i <= 10; ++i) {
        std::this_thread::sleep_for(std::chrono::milliseconds(50));
         // Simulate order generation time
        std::unique_lock<std::mutex> lock(orderMutex);
        orderQueue.push(i);  // Add order to the queue
```

CHAPTER 7: REAL-WORLD APPLICATIONS OF C++ CONCURRENCY

```
        lock.unlock();  // Unlock after adding the order
        std::cout << "Generated order: " << i << std::endl;
    }
    done = true;  // Indicate that order generation is done
}

int main() {
    std::thread processor(processOrders);
    std::thread generator(generateOrders);

    processor.join();
    generator.join();

    return 0;
}
```

In this implementation:

- The processOrders function processes orders from the queue.
- The generateOrders function simulates the generation of incoming orders.
- Mutexes are used to synchronize access to the shared order queue.

5. Scientific Computing and Concurrency

Scientific computing often involves processing large datasets and performing complex calculations. Concurrency can significantly speed up simulations and data processing tasks by distributing workloads across multiple threads or cores.

5.1 Overview of Scientific Computing Workflows

A typical scientific computing workflow may include:

- **Data Acquisition**: Gathering data from experiments or simulations.
- **Data Processing**: Analyzing and processing the collected data.
- **Simulations**: Running simulations that require significant computational resources.

- **Visualization**: Generating visual representations of data or simulation results.

5.2 Implementing Parallel Data Processing

Let's implement a simple example of parallel data processing using C++ threads and atomic operations.

Example: Parallel Data Processing

```cpp
Copy code
#include <iostream>
#include <thread>
#include <vector>
#include <numeric>
#include <atomic>

std::atomic<int> totalSum(0);  // Atomic variable for storing the total sum

void computePartialSum(const std::vector<int>& data, int start, int end) {
    int sum = std::accumulate(data.begin() + start, data.begin() + end, 0);
    totalSum += sum;  // Add to the total sum
}

int main() {
    const int dataSize = 10000;
    std::vector<int> data(dataSize);
    std::iota(data.begin(), data.end(), 1);  // Fill with numbers 1 to 10000

    const int numThreads = 4;
    std::vector<std::thread> threads;
    int chunkSize = dataSize / numThreads;

    for (int i = 0; i < numThreads; ++i) {
        int start = i * chunkSize;
```

```
        int end = (i == numThreads - 1) ? dataSize : start +
        chunkSize;  // Handle last chunk
        threads.emplace_back(computePartialSum, std::ref(data),
        start, end);
    }

    for (auto& t : threads) {
        t.join();  // Wait for all threads to finish
    }

    std::cout << "Total sum: " << totalSum << std::endl;

    return 0;
}
```

In this example:

- We create a vector filled with numbers from 1 to 10,000.
- We split the data into chunks and process each chunk in parallel using threads.
- An atomic variable is used to maintain a running total of the sums calculated by each thread.

6. Summary of Real-World Applications

In this chapter, we explored various real-world applications of C++ concurrency, including:

- **Multithreaded web servers**: Handling multiple client requests simultaneously.
- **Game development**: Managing rendering and input handling concurrently.
- **Financial systems**: Processing transactions and market data in real time.
- **Scientific computing**: Parallelizing data processing tasks to improve performance.

By applying the concurrency concepts and design patterns discussed throughout this book, you can build robust, high-performance applications in diverse domains. Understanding these applications provides valuable insights into the practical use of concurrency in C++.

7. Conclusion

As we conclude this chapter, it's clear that concurrency is a vital component of modern software development. By leveraging the power of multithreading and applying appropriate design patterns, you can create applications that are efficient, scalable, and responsive. In the next chapter, we will explore **advanced topics in C++ concurrency**, including performance tuning, profiling tools, and best practices for maintaining thread safety in complex systems.

Chapter 8: Advanced Topics in C++ Concurrency

In this chapter, we will delve into advanced topics in C++ concurrency, focusing on performance tuning, profiling tools, and best practices for writing robust multithreaded applications. Understanding these topics is essential for developing high-performance systems that can effectively utilize multicore processors. This chapter aims to equip you with the knowledge necessary to optimize your concurrent applications, identify bottlenecks, and ensure thread safety while maintaining code clarity and maintainability.

1. Introduction to Advanced Concurrency Concepts

Concurrency in C++ is a powerful tool that, when used correctly, can lead to significant performance improvements. However, achieving optimal performance and robustness in multithreaded applications requires an understanding of various advanced topics. This chapter will cover:

- Performance tuning strategies for concurrent applications.
- Profiling tools and techniques to identify bottlenecks and optimize thread usage.
- Best practices for maintaining thread safety and code quality in complex

systems.

1.1 Goals of Advanced Concurrency

The goals of studying advanced concurrency topics include:

- **Enhancing Performance**: Identifying and eliminating bottlenecks to ensure that your application runs efficiently.
- **Ensuring Robustness**: Preventing common concurrency issues like deadlocks, race conditions, and memory consistency errors.
- **Improving Code Quality**: Writing clear, maintainable code that leverages concurrency effectively.

2. Performance Tuning for Concurrent Applications

Performance tuning involves optimizing the efficiency of concurrent applications. This section will discuss various strategies and techniques that can be employed to enhance the performance of multithreaded programs.

2.1 Minimizing Lock Contention

Lock contention occurs when multiple threads compete for the same lock, leading to delays and reduced performance. To minimize lock contention:

- **Use Fine-Grained Locks**: Instead of locking a large section of code, use multiple smaller locks to protect different shared resources. This allows threads to access non-conflicting resources simultaneously.
- **Reduce Lock Scope**: Keep the code within critical sections as short as possible. Lock only the parts of the code that actually need to be synchronized.
- **Avoid Locking for Read-Only Operations**: If a resource is read-only, consider using atomic operations or shared locks to allow concurrent reads without locking.

Example: Fine-Grained Locking

CHAPTER 8: ADVANCED TOPICS IN C++ CONCURRENCY

```cpp
Copy code
#include <iostream>
#include <thread>
#include <vector>
#include <mutex>

std::mutex mtx1, mtx2;   // Two mutexes for fine-grained locking
int sharedData1 = 0;
int sharedData2 = 0;

void incrementData1() {
    for (int i = 0; i < 1000; ++i) {
        std::lock_guard<std::mutex> lock(mtx1);
        ++sharedData1;
    }
}

void incrementData2() {
    for (int i = 0; i < 1000; ++i) {
        std::lock_guard<std::mutex> lock(mtx2);
        ++sharedData2;
    }
}

int main() {
    std::thread t1(incrementData1);
    std::thread t2(incrementData2);

    t1.join();
    t2.join();

    std::cout << "Final sharedData1: " << sharedData1 << std::endl;
    std::cout << "Final sharedData2: " << sharedData2 << std::endl;

    return 0;
}
```

In this example, two separate mutexes (mtx1 and mtx2) are used to protect different shared resources. This allows both threads to operate concurrently without contention.

2.2 Optimizing Thread Usage

Optimizing thread usage is crucial for achieving high performance. Strategies include:

- **Thread Pooling**: Use a thread pool to manage a fixed number of threads that can be reused for executing tasks. This reduces the overhead of thread creation and destruction.
- **Dynamic Thread Management**: Implement dynamic thread management to adjust the number of active threads based on the workload. For example, increase the number of threads during peak times and decrease during idle periods.

2.3 Load Balancing

Load balancing ensures that work is distributed evenly among threads to avoid scenarios where some threads are overworked while others are idle. Techniques include:

- **Work Stealing**: In work-stealing, idle threads can "steal" work from busy threads, ensuring a balanced workload.
- **Task Scheduling**: Use intelligent scheduling algorithms to assign tasks to threads based on their current workload and resource availability.

Example: Simple Load Balancing Using a Thread Pool

```cpp
Copy code
#include <iostream>
#include <thread>
#include <vector>
#include <queue>
#include <condition_variable>
#include <functional>
```

CHAPTER 8: ADVANCED TOPICS IN C++ CONCURRENCY

```cpp
class ThreadPool {
public:
    ThreadPool(size_t numThreads);
    ~ThreadPool();
    void enqueue(std::function<void()> task);

private:
    std::vector<std::thread> workers;
    std::queue<std::function<void()>> tasks;
    std::mutex mtx;
    std::condition_variable cv;
    bool stop;

    void worker();
};

ThreadPool::ThreadPool(size_t numThreads) : stop(false) {
    for (size_t i = 0; i < numThreads; ++i) {
        workers.emplace_back([this] { this->worker(); });
    }
}

ThreadPool::~ThreadPool() {
    stop = true;
    cv.notify_all();   // Wake up all threads
    for (std::thread& worker : workers) {
        worker.join();   // Wait for all threads to finish
    }
}

void ThreadPool::enqueue(std::function<void()> task) {
    {
        std::lock_guard<std::mutex> lock(mtx);
        tasks.push(std::move(task));
    }
    cv.notify_one();   // Notify one waiting thread
}

void ThreadPool::worker() {
    while (true) {
```

```cpp
            std::function<void()> task;

            {
                std::unique_lock<std::mutex> lock(mtx);
                cv.wait(lock, [this] { return stop || !tasks.empty();
                });
                if (stop && tasks.empty()) return;   // Exit if stopping
                task = std::move(tasks.front());
                tasks.pop();
            }

            task();  // Execute the task
        }
    }
}

void exampleTask(int id) {
    std::cout << "Task " << id << " is being processed." <<
    std::endl;
}

int main() {
    ThreadPool pool(4);   // Create a thread pool with 4 threads

    // Enqueue tasks
    for (int i = 0; i < 10; ++i) {
        pool.enqueue([i] { exampleTask(i); });
    }

    return 0;
}
```

In this thread pool implementation, tasks are distributed among a fixed number of worker threads, ensuring efficient load balancing and resource utilization.

3. Profiling Tools and Techniques

Profiling is essential for identifying performance bottlenecks in multithreaded applications. This section discusses various profiling tools and techniques that can help you analyze thread behavior and resource usage.

3.1 Overview of Profiling

Profiling involves measuring the performance of an application to identify areas for optimization. In the context of multithreading, profiling can reveal:

- **Thread Contention**: Identifying which threads are frequently competing for locks.
- **CPU Usage**: Understanding how CPU resources are being utilized by different threads.
- **Response Times**: Measuring the time taken to execute various tasks and identifying slow operations.

3.2 Popular Profiling Tools

Several tools are available for profiling C++ applications, each with its strengths and weaknesses. Here are some popular options:

1. **gprof**: A profiling tool for C/C++ programs that provides a call graph and execution time statistics.
2. **Valgrind**: A tool for memory debugging and profiling that can detect memory leaks and track memory usage.
3. **perf**: A powerful Linux tool for profiling and analyzing performance on a low level, including CPU cycles and cache misses.
4. **Visual Studio Profiler**: An integrated profiling tool for applications developed with Microsoft Visual Studio, offering detailed performance analysis.

3.3 Profiling Techniques

When profiling multithreaded applications, consider the following techniques:

- **Thread Profiling**: Measure the performance of individual threads, including execution time, CPU usage, and context switch counts.
- **Lock Contention Analysis**: Identify which locks are causing contention and evaluate their impact on performance.
- **Function Call Analysis**: Measure the time spent in different functions to identify slow or frequently called functions.

4. Best Practices for Writing Robust Concurrent Code

Writing concurrent code requires careful consideration to ensure that it is robust and maintainable. This section outlines best practices to help you avoid common pitfalls and produce high-quality concurrent applications.

4.1 Keep Code Simple and Readable

- **Minimize Complexity**: Aim to keep your concurrent code simple and straightforward. Complex synchronization can lead to bugs and make your code harder to maintain.
- **Use Meaningful Names**: Use descriptive names for threads, functions, and variables to convey their purpose and improve code readability.

4.2 Document Threading Behavior

- **Document Thread Safety**: Clearly indicate which functions are thread-safe and which are not. Provide guidelines on how to use shared resources safely.
- **Comment Synchronization Logic**: Add comments to explain the purpose and behavior of locks, condition variables, and other synchronization mechanisms.

4.3 Avoid Shared State When Possible

- **Immutable Data**: Use immutable data structures wherever feasible. If a data structure does not change, multiple threads can access it safely

without synchronization.
- **Message Passing**: Consider using message-passing techniques instead of shared state to communicate between threads. This can simplify synchronization and improve modularity.

4.4 Test for Concurrency Issues

- **Stress Testing**: Use stress testing to identify concurrency issues under heavy load. Test how your application behaves with many threads running simultaneously.
- **Race Condition Detection**: Use tools and libraries designed to detect race conditions, such as ThreadSanitizer, which can help catch concurrency bugs during development.

4.5 Regular Code Reviews

Conduct regular code reviews focusing on concurrent code. Reviewers should check for proper synchronization, potential deadlocks, and adherence to best practices. Peer feedback can be invaluable for catching issues early.

5. Performance Optimization Techniques

Optimizing the performance of concurrent applications is essential for achieving the desired responsiveness and throughput. This section discusses several techniques for optimizing performance in C++ concurrency.

5.1 Measuring and Analyzing Performance

Before optimizing, measure the performance of your application using profiling tools. Analyze the collected data to identify bottlenecks and areas for improvement. Focus on optimizing the most critical sections of your code.

5.2 Reducing Context Switches

Excessive context switching can degrade performance. To minimize context switches:

- **Limit the Number of Threads**: Keep the number of active threads in line with the number of available CPU cores.
- **Use Task-Based Parallelism**: Instead of creating many threads, consider using a task-based approach where tasks are dynamically assigned to a limited number of threads.

5.3 Cache Optimization

Memory access patterns can significantly impact performance due to cache locality. To optimize cache usage:

- **Data Locality**: Structure your data to maximize spatial and temporal locality. Group related data together in memory to improve cache performance.
- **Thread Affinity**: Bind threads to specific CPU cores to take advantage of CPU caches and reduce cache misses.

5.4 Efficient Use of Synchronization Primitives

- **Lock-Free Algorithms**: When possible, use lock-free algorithms to eliminate the overhead associated with locks and improve throughput.
- **Adaptive Locking**: Implement adaptive locking strategies that change the locking mechanism based on the contention level, switching between spinlocks and mutexes as needed.

6. Conclusion

In this chapter, we explored advanced topics in C++ concurrency, including performance tuning, profiling tools, and best practices for writing robust concurrent code. We discussed strategies for minimizing lock contention, optimizing thread usage, and implementing effective load balancing. Additionally, we highlighted the importance of profiling and testing to identify bottlenecks and concurrency issues.

By mastering these advanced concepts and techniques, you can develop high-performance, scalable, and maintainable concurrent applications in C++. In the next chapter, we will focus on **case studies and real-world examples**, applying the principles and patterns discussed throughout this book to practical scenarios in various domains.

Chapter 9: Case Studies and Real-World Examples in C++ Concurrency

In this chapter, we will explore various case studies and real-world examples that demonstrate the practical application of concurrency concepts in C++. By examining different domains, we will see how multithreading and synchronization patterns can be effectively utilized to solve complex problems. Each case study will provide insights into the design decisions made, the challenges faced, and the performance considerations taken into account.

1. Introduction to Case Studies

Understanding concurrency through theoretical concepts is essential, but applying these concepts to real-world problems is where the true value lies. In this chapter, we will cover a range of case studies, including:

- A multithreaded image processing application.
- A simulation of a banking system for handling transactions.
- A scientific computing application for large data analysis.
- A real-time chat application using C++.

By analyzing these examples, you will gain a deeper understanding of how to implement concurrency in practical scenarios, addressing common challenges and optimizing for performance.

2. Case Study 1: Multithreaded Image Processing

In the realm of image processing, tasks such as filtering, resizing, and transforming images can be computationally intensive. By leveraging concurrency, we can significantly reduce the time taken to process images by dividing tasks across multiple threads.

2.1 Overview of the Image Processing Application

The application will perform several operations on images:

- **Loading Images**: Read images from disk.
- **Processing**: Apply filters and transformations concurrently.
- **Saving Images**: Write processed images back to disk.

2.2 Designing the Multithreaded Image Processing Application

The design involves:

- **Thread Pool**: To manage a fixed number of worker threads that process image tasks.
- **Task Queue**: To hold pending image processing tasks.
- **Synchronization**: Use mutexes to synchronize access to shared resources (e.g., the task queue).

Example: Multithreaded Image Processing Implementation

```cpp
Copy code
#include <iostream>
#include <thread>
#include <mutex>
#include <vector>
```

```cpp
#include <queue>
#include <condition_variable>
#include <string>
#include <opencv2/opencv.hpp> // OpenCV for image processing

class ThreadPool {
public:
    ThreadPool(size_t numThreads);
    ~ThreadPool();
    void enqueue(std::function<void()> task);

private:
    std::vector<std::thread> workers;
    std::queue<std::function<void()>> tasks;
    std::mutex mtx;
    std::condition_variable cv;
    bool stop;

    void worker();
};

ThreadPool::ThreadPool(size_t numThreads) : stop(false) {
    for (size_t i = 0; i < numThreads; ++i) {
        workers.emplace_back([this] { this->worker(); });
    }
}

ThreadPool::~ThreadPool() {
    stop = true;
    cv.notify_all();
    for (std::thread& worker : workers) {
        worker.join();
    }
}

void ThreadPool::enqueue(std::function<void()> task) {
    {
        std::lock_guard<std::mutex> lock(mtx);
        tasks.push(std::move(task));
    }
```

CHAPTER 9: CASE STUDIES AND REAL-WORLD EXAMPLES IN C++...

```cpp
        cv.notify_one();
}

void ThreadPool::worker() {
    while (true) {
        std::function<void()> task;

        {
            std::unique_lock<std::mutex> lock(mtx);
            cv.wait(lock, [this] { return stop || !tasks.empty();
            });
            if (stop && tasks.empty()) return;
            task = std::move(tasks.front());
            tasks.pop();
        }

        task();
    }
}

void processImage(const std::string& imagePath) {
    cv::Mat image = cv::imread(imagePath);
    if (image.empty()) {
        std::cerr << "Error: Could not load image " << imagePath
        << std::endl;
        return;
    }

    // Apply a simple filter (Gaussian Blur)
    cv::GaussianBlur(image, image, cv::Size(5, 5), 0);

    // Save the processed image
    cv::imwrite("processed_" + imagePath, image);
    std::cout << "Processed image: " << imagePath << std::endl;
}

int main() {
    ThreadPool pool(4);   // Create a thread pool with 4 threads

    std::vector<std::string> imagePaths = {
```

```
        "image1.jpg", "image2.jpg", "image3.jpg", // Add your
        image paths here
    };

    for (const auto& path : imagePaths) {
        pool.enqueue([path] { processImage(path); });
    }

    return 0;
}
```

In this example:

- A thread pool manages a fixed number of worker threads.
- Each thread processes an image by applying a Gaussian blur filter using OpenCV.
- The application loads images, processes them concurrently, and saves the results.

2.3 Performance Considerations

When optimizing the performance of the image processing application, consider:

- **Chunk Size**: Dividing large images into smaller chunks to improve parallelism.
- **Efficient Resource Management**: Using a thread pool minimizes the overhead of thread creation and destruction.
- **Load Balancing**: Ensuring that all threads have an equal amount of work to prevent some threads from being idle while others are busy.

CHAPTER 9: CASE STUDIES AND REAL-WORLD EXAMPLES IN C++...

3. Case Study 2: Banking System Simulation

A banking system is an excellent example of a concurrent application that requires managing multiple transactions simultaneously. This case study will simulate a simple banking system where multiple clients can deposit and withdraw funds concurrently.

3.1 Overview of the Banking System Simulation

The system will handle the following operations:

- **Deposits**: Clients can deposit money into their accounts.
- **Withdrawals**: Clients can withdraw money from their accounts.
- **Balance Inquiry**: Clients can check their account balance.

3.2 Designing the Banking System Simulation

The design includes:

- **Account Class**: Represents a bank account with methods for deposits, withdrawals, and balance inquiries.
- **Mutex for Synchronization**: Ensures thread-safe access to account data.

Example: Banking System Simulation Implementation

```cpp
Copy code
#include <iostream>
#include <thread>
#include <mutex>
#include <vector>
#include <chrono>

class BankAccount {
public:
    BankAccount(int initialBalance) : balance(initialBalance) {}
```

```cpp
    void deposit(int amount) {
        std::lock_guard<std::mutex> lock(mtx);
        balance += amount;
        std::cout << "Deposited: " << amount << ", New Balance: "
        << balance << std::endl;
    }

    void withdraw(int amount) {
        std::lock_guard<std::mutex> lock(mtx);
        if (amount <= balance) {
            balance -= amount;
            std::cout << "Withdrew: " << amount << ", New Balance:
            " << balance << std::endl;
        } else {
            std::cout << "Withdrawal of " << amount << " failed,
            insufficient funds!" << std::endl;
        }
    }

    int getBalance() {
        std::lock_guard<std::mutex> lock(mtx);
        return balance;
    }

private:
    int balance;
    std::mutex mtx;   // Mutex for synchronizing access
};

void client(BankAccount& account) {
    account.deposit(100);
    account.withdraw(50);
    std::cout << "Client balance: " << account.getBalance() <<
    std::endl;
}

int main() {
    BankAccount account(500);   // Initial balance
```

CHAPTER 9: CASE STUDIES AND REAL-WORLD EXAMPLES IN C++...

```cpp
    const int numClients = 5;
    std::vector<std::thread> clients;

    // Create client threads
    for (int i = 0; i < numClients; ++i) {
        clients.emplace_back(client, std::ref(account));
    }

    // Wait for all clients to finish
    for (auto& c : clients) {
        c.join();
    }

    return 0;
}
```

In this implementation:

- The BankAccount class encapsulates account operations, ensuring thread-safe access using mutexes.
- The client function simulates a bank client performing deposit and withdrawal operations.
- Multiple client threads interact with the same BankAccount instance concurrently.

3.3 Performance Considerations

Key considerations for optimizing the banking system simulation:

- **Granularity of Locks**: Consider using finer-grained locks if accounts have shared resources to reduce contention.
- **Concurrency Control**: Implementing optimistic locking or transactions can improve performance by reducing the need for locks when accessing shared resources.

4. Case Study 3: Scientific Computing Application

Scientific computing often involves processing large datasets and performing complex calculations. This case study will demonstrate how concurrency can be leveraged to speed up data analysis and simulations in a scientific computing application.

4.1 Overview of the Scientific Computing Application

The application will perform the following tasks:

- **Data Acquisition**: Simulating the collection of large datasets.
- **Parallel Processing**: Analyzing data using multiple threads to speed up calculations.
- **Results Aggregation**: Combining results from multiple threads.

4.2 Designing the Scientific Computing Application

The design involves:

- **Data Structure**: A structure to hold the dataset.
- **Worker Threads**: Threads that process chunks of the dataset concurrently.
- **Synchronization Mechanism**: Using mutexes to aggregate results safely.

Example: Scientific Computing Application Implementation

```cpp
Copy code
#include <iostream>
#include <thread>
#include <vector>
#include <atomic>
#include <cmath>
#include <chrono>
```

CHAPTER 9: CASE STUDIES AND REAL-WORLD EXAMPLES IN C++...

```cpp
const int dataSize = 1000000;  // Size of the dataset
std::vector<double> data(dataSize);  // Dataset
std::atomic<double> totalSum(0);  // Atomic variable for the total sum

void computePartialSum(int start, int end) {
    double sum = 0;
    for (int i = start; i < end; ++i) {
        sum += std::sqrt(data[i]);  // Example computation
    }
    totalSum += sum;  // Add to the total sum atomically
}

int main() {
    // Initialize the dataset
    for (int i = 0; i < dataSize; ++i) {
        data[i] = static_cast<double>(i);
    }

    const int numThreads = 4;
    std::vector<std::thread> threads;
    int chunkSize = dataSize / numThreads;

    // Start processing in parallel
    for (int i = 0; i < numThreads; ++i) {
        int start = i * chunkSize;
        int end = (i == numThreads - 1) ? dataSize : start + chunkSize;
        threads.emplace_back(computePartialSum, start, end);
    }

    // Wait for all threads to finish
    for (auto& t : threads) {
        t.join();
    }

    std::cout << "Total sum: " << totalSum << std::endl;

    return 0;
}
```

In this implementation:

- The application computes the sum of the square roots of a large dataset in parallel.
- Each thread processes a chunk of the data, and results are combined using an atomic variable to ensure thread safety.

4.3 Performance Considerations

When optimizing the scientific computing application:

- **Data Locality**: Structure the data to improve cache usage and minimize cache misses.
- **Efficient Thread Management**: Use a thread pool to manage threads more efficiently if the workload fluctuates.
- **Load Balancing**: Ensure that each thread has a roughly equal amount of work to maximize CPU utilization.

5. Case Study 4: Real-Time Chat Application

Real-time applications like chat systems require low latency and high responsiveness. This case study will demonstrate how to implement a simple multithreaded chat application using C++.

5.1 Overview of the Chat Application

The chat application will have the following features:

- **Multiple Clients**: Support multiple clients connecting to the server.
- **Message Broadcasting**: Broadcast messages from one client to all other connected clients.
- **Thread Management**: Use threads to handle each client connection.

5.2 Designing the Chat Application

The design involves:

- **Server**: A multithreaded server that listens for incoming connections.
- **Client Handling**: Each client connection is managed in a separate thread.
- **Message Queue**: A shared queue to manage incoming messages.

Example: Real-Time Chat Application Implementation

```cpp
Copy code
#include <iostream>
#include <thread>
#include <mutex>
#include <vector>
#include <queue>
#include <condition_variable>
#include <string>
#include <cstring>
#include <arpa/inet.h>
#include <unistd.h>

std::vector<int> clients;    // Vector to store client sockets
std::mutex clientsMutex;     // Mutex for synchronizing access to clients
std::queue<std::string> messageQueue;  // Message queue
std::mutex messageMutex;     // Mutex for message queue
std::condition_variable cv;  // Condition variable for signaling

void broadcastMessage(const std::string& message) {
    std::lock_guard<std::mutex> lock(clientsMutex);
    for (int client : clients) {
        send(client, message.c_str(), message.size(), 0);
    }
}

void handleClient(int clientSocket) {
    char buffer[1024];
    while (true) {
        std::memset(buffer, 0, sizeof(buffer));
        int bytesReceived = recv(clientSocket, buffer, sizeof(buffer), 0);
```

```cpp
            if (bytesReceived <= 0) {
                break;   // Client disconnected
            }
            std::string message(buffer);

            // Broadcast the received message
            {
                std::lock_guard<std::mutex> lock(messageMutex);
                messageQueue.push(message);
            }
            cv.notify_all();  // Notify other threads that a new
            message has arrived
        }

        // Remove the client from the list
        {
            std::lock_guard<std::mutex> lock(clientsMutex);
            clients.erase(std::remove(clients.begin(), clients.end(),
            clientSocket), clients.end());
        }
        close(clientSocket);
}

void messageHandler() {
    while (true) {
        std::unique_lock<std::mutex> lock(messageMutex);
        cv.wait(lock, [] { return !messageQueue.empty(); });

        while (!messageQueue.empty()) {
            std::string message = messageQueue.front();
            messageQueue.pop();
            broadcastMessage(message);
        }
    }
}

void serverLoop(int port) {
    int serverSocket, clientSocket;
    struct sockaddr_in serverAddr, clientAddr;
    socklen_t clientAddrLen = sizeof(clientAddr);
```

```cpp
    // Create socket
    serverSocket = socket(AF_INET, SOCK_STREAM, 0);
    serverAddr.sin_family = AF_INET;
    serverAddr.sin_addr.s_addr = INADDR_ANY;
    serverAddr.sin_port = htons(port);

    // Bind the socket
    bind(serverSocket, (struct sockaddr*)&serverAddr,
    sizeof(serverAddr));
    listen(serverSocket, 5);    // Listen for incoming connections

    std::cout << "Chat server is listening on port " << port <<
    std::endl;

    while (true) {
        // Accept a client connection
        clientSocket = accept(serverSocket, (struct
        sockaddr*)&clientAddr, &clientAddrLen);

        {
            std::lock_guard<std::mutex> lock(clientsMutex);
            clients.push_back(clientSocket);
        }

        // Spawn a new thread to handle the client
        std::thread(handleClient, clientSocket).detach();
    }

    close(serverSocket);
}

int main() {
    std::thread msgHandler(messageHandler);   // Start the message
    handler thread
    serverLoop(8080);  // Start the server loop on port 8080
    msgHandler.join();  // Wait for the message handler to finish
    return 0;
}
```

In this implementation:

- The server listens for incoming client connections and spawns a new thread to handle each client.
- Each client can send messages that are broadcasted to all other connected clients.
- The application uses mutexes and condition variables to manage access to shared resources (client list and message queue).

5.3 Performance Considerations

When optimizing the real-time chat application:

- **Connection Management**: Efficiently manage a large number of client connections.
- **Message Queuing**: Optimize message queuing and broadcasting to minimize latency.
- **Scalability**: Design the server to handle increased load by using a thread pool or asynchronous I/O.

6. Conclusion

In this chapter, we explored various case studies and real-world examples of applying C++ concurrency concepts. We covered:

- A multithreaded image processing application that utilizes a thread pool for concurrent processing.
- A banking system simulation demonstrating thread-safe operations on shared resources.
- A scientific computing application that performs parallel data processing.
- A real-time chat application showcasing client handling and message broadcasting.

By analyzing these case studies, you can see how concurrency patterns and best practices can be effectively implemented to solve practical problems across different domains. The knowledge gained from these examples will equip you to tackle your own concurrency challenges in C++ programming.

In the next chapter, we will conclude this book with final thoughts on C++ concurrency, summarizing the key concepts and looking ahead to future developments in multithreading and parallel programming.

Chapter 10: Final Thoughts on C++ Concurrency

As we conclude this exploration of concurrency in C++, it's essential to reflect on the knowledge and techniques we've covered, their practical applications, and the future of multithreading and parallel programming. This chapter will summarize the key concepts learned, discuss the challenges faced by developers in concurrent programming, and provide insights into emerging trends and technologies in the field of C++ concurrency.

1. Summary of Key Concepts

Concurrency in C++ provides powerful tools for creating efficient and responsive applications that can take full advantage of modern multicore processors. Here, we will summarize the essential topics covered throughout this book.

1.1 Basics of Concurrency

We began by establishing the foundational concepts of concurrency and parallelism, highlighting the differences between the two and emphasizing the importance of multithreading in performance optimization. Understanding these distinctions is critical for applying the right approach to a given problem.

- **Concurrency** allows multiple tasks to progress simultaneously, potentially sharing resources.
- **Parallelism** refers to executing multiple tasks at the same time, typically on different CPU cores.

1.2 C++ Concurrency Support

We examined the concurrency support provided by C++, which includes the <thread>, <mutex>, and <future> libraries. C++11 introduced these standard libraries, enabling developers to easily create and manage threads, synchronize access to shared resources, and handle asynchronous operations.

- **Threads**: The std::thread class facilitates the creation and management of threads.
- **Mutexes**: Synchronization primitives like std::mutex and std::lock_guard help prevent race conditions.
- **Condition Variables**: The std::condition_variable class allows threads to wait for specific conditions before proceeding.

1.3 Synchronization Mechanisms

We discussed various synchronization mechanisms that prevent data races and ensure data integrity in multithreaded applications. These include:

- **Mutexes**: Used to protect shared resources from concurrent access.
- **Condition Variables**: Allow threads to wait for conditions and signal other threads when conditions are met.
- **Atomic Operations**: Enable lock-free access to shared variables, improving performance in certain scenarios.

1.4 Concurrency Design Patterns

Several design patterns facilitate effective concurrency. We explored the following:

- **Producer-Consumer Pattern**: Manages the flow of data between

producers and consumers, ensuring efficient use of resources.
- **Reader-Writer Pattern**: Allows multiple readers or a single writer to access shared resources, optimizing read-heavy workloads.
- **Future and Promise Pattern**: Enables asynchronous programming by allowing a thread to produce a value that can be retrieved later.

1.5 Advanced Topics

In the advanced topics section, we discussed performance tuning, profiling tools, and best practices for writing robust concurrent code. Key points include:

- **Minimizing Lock Contention**: Use fine-grained locks and reduce lock scope to enhance performance.
- **Profiling**: Utilize tools to identify bottlenecks and analyze thread behavior.
- **Testing for Concurrency Issues**: Stress test applications to detect race conditions and deadlocks.

2. Challenges in Concurrent Programming

Despite the powerful features and capabilities of C++, concurrent programming comes with its challenges. These challenges can complicate development and impact the reliability of applications. Some of the key challenges include:

2.1 Complexity of Multithreaded Code

Concurrency adds complexity to code, making it harder to understand and maintain. Developers must carefully manage thread lifecycles, synchronization, and data sharing, which can lead to bugs and unintended behavior.

2.2 Race Conditions and Deadlocks

Race conditions occur when multiple threads access shared data simultaneously, leading to inconsistent results. Deadlocks happen when two or more threads are waiting for each other to release resources, causing the program to hang. Detecting and resolving these issues can be challenging.

2.3 Debugging Multithreaded Applications

Debugging multithreaded applications is often more complicated than debugging single-threaded programs. Issues like race conditions may not manifest consistently, making them difficult to reproduce and fix.

2.4 Performance Trade-offs

While concurrency can improve performance, improper use can lead to performance degradation. For example, excessive locking can introduce bottlenecks, and too many threads can lead to increased context switching.

3. The Future of C++ Concurrency

The field of concurrency is constantly evolving, with new techniques, tools, and paradigms emerging. Several trends are shaping the future of C++ concurrency:

3.1 Ongoing Language Improvements

C++ continues to evolve, with each new standard introducing features that enhance concurrency support. For instance, C++20 introduced concepts such as coroutines, which simplify asynchronous programming by allowing developers to write asynchronous code in a more natural and readable manner.

3.2 Growing Use of Functional Programming Paradigms

Functional programming paradigms are gaining traction in C++. Concepts like immutability and higher-order functions can help reduce side effects and make concurrent programming easier. Libraries such as Boost and C++ standard libraries are beginning to incorporate functional programming principles.

3.3 Increased Focus on Parallel Algorithms

The C++ Standard Library is increasingly adopting parallel algorithms, enabling developers to express parallelism at a higher level of abstraction. Features like std::for_each and std::transform can be executed in parallel, simplifying the implementation of concurrent algorithms.

3.4 Enhancements in Tools and Libraries

The development of advanced profiling and debugging tools continues to improve the ability to analyze and optimize concurrent applications. Tools that provide insights into thread behavior, resource usage, and performance metrics are essential for developing robust concurrent systems.

4. Practical Recommendations for Developers

As you continue your journey in C++ concurrency, consider the following practical recommendations to enhance your development practices:

4.1 Embrace Concurrency Early in Development

Incorporate concurrency early in the design phase of your application. Identify which components can benefit from parallelism and plan for synchronization and data sharing from the start.

4.2 Keep Learning and Experimenting

Concurrency is a complex topic that requires ongoing learning. Stay updated with new developments in C++, libraries, and concurrency patterns. Experiment with different approaches to solve concurrency challenges.

4.3 Contribute to Open Source Projects

Participating in open-source projects that focus on C++ concurrency can provide valuable experience. Contributing to collaborative projects allows you to learn from others and share your insights.

4.4 Use Existing Libraries

Take advantage of existing libraries that offer robust concurrency features. Libraries such as Intel TBB, OpenMP, and Boost provide powerful abstractions for managing concurrency and parallelism.

5. Conclusion

As we conclude this exploration of concurrency in C++, it is evident that mastering concurrent programming is essential for building high-performance, responsive applications in today's multicore world. This chapter summarized the key concepts covered throughout the book and highlighted the challenges developers face in concurrent programming.

We also discussed the future of C++ concurrency and provided practical recommendations to help you navigate the complexities of multithreading. By leveraging the principles, patterns, and tools presented in this book, you will be well-equipped to tackle the challenges of concurrency in your projects.

As you embark on your journey with C++ concurrency, remember that practice and experimentation are key. Each application presents unique challenges and opportunities, and with the knowledge gained in this book, you have the tools to succeed in developing robust and efficient concurrent applications.

6. Looking Ahead

The realm of C++ concurrency is ever-evolving, with new standards and technologies continually being developed. As you move forward, stay engaged with the community, explore new resources, and continue to enhance your skills in this critical area of software development. The future holds exciting opportunities for those who master concurrency in C++, and your journey has just begun.

Chapter 11: Best Practices and Design Guidelines for C++ Concurrency

Concurrency in C++ is a powerful tool for developing high-performance applications, but it comes with complexities that require careful consideration. In this chapter, we will explore best practices and design guidelines that can help developers effectively leverage concurrency while avoiding common pitfalls. By following these guidelines, you will enhance the robustness, maintainability, and performance of your concurrent applications.

1. Introduction to Best Practices in C++ Concurrency

The effective use of concurrency involves understanding the principles that govern multithreaded programming. This chapter will cover essential best practices and design guidelines, including:

- Structuring concurrent code for clarity and maintainability.
- Managing resources and synchronization effectively.
- Optimizing performance while ensuring thread safety.
- Testing and debugging multithreaded applications.

These practices will help you build applications that are not only efficient

2. Structuring Concurrent Code

A clear and organized code structure is vital for managing the complexity of concurrent programming. Here are some best practices for structuring your concurrent C++ code.

2.1 Use Meaningful Names

Choosing meaningful names for variables, functions, and classes enhances code readability. When working with concurrency, consider including the following in your naming conventions:

- Indicate thread-related functionalities (e.g., processInThread, sharedDataMutex).
- Use consistent naming conventions that reflect the purpose of the code.

Example:

```cpp
Copy code
std::mutex sharedResourceMutex;  // Clearly indicates the purpose
of the mutex
```

2.2 Keep Functions Short and Focused

Long functions that handle multiple responsibilities can introduce complexity and make debugging difficult. Instead, aim for short, focused functions that perform a single task.

Example:

Instead of combining several tasks in a single function:

```cpp
Copy code
void handleClient() {
    // Multiple responsibilities, such as reading data, processing
```

it, and sending a response.
}

Break it down into smaller, focused functions:

```cpp
Copy code
void readData();
void processData();
void sendResponse();
```

2.3 Use RAII for Resource Management

Resource Acquisition Is Initialization (RAII) is a programming idiom that binds the lifecycle of resources to the lifetime of objects. Using RAII for managing resources like locks ensures that they are automatically released when the object goes out of scope, reducing the risk of deadlocks.

Example:

Using std::lock_guard for mutex management:

```cpp
Copy code
void updateSharedResource() {
    std::lock_guard<std::mutex> lock(mtx);  // Automatically
    unlocks when going out of scope
    // Update shared resource here
}
```

3. Managing Resources and Synchronization

Proper management of resources and synchronization is critical in concurrent programming to prevent issues such as race conditions and deadlocks.

3.1 Use the Appropriate Synchronization Primitives

Choose the right synchronization mechanisms based on your specific needs:

- **Mutexes**: Use for protecting shared resources that require exclusive access.
- **Condition Variables**: Use for signaling between threads.
- **Atomic Operations**: Use for simple shared variables that need lock-free access.

Example: Using Atomic Operations

```cpp
Copy code
std::atomic<int> counter(0);   // Atomic integer

void increment() {
    ++counter;   // Thread-safe increment
}
```

3.2 Minimize the Scope of Locks

Keep the code within critical sections as short as possible to reduce lock contention. Only lock the parts of the code that need access to shared resources.

Example:

Instead of locking a large block of code:

```cpp
Copy code
void criticalSection() {
    std::lock_guard<std::mutex> lock(mtx);
    // Do some work...
    // Do more work...
}
```

Limit the lock to the specific operations that need it:

```cpp
Copy code
void criticalSection() {
    {
        std::lock_guard<std::mutex> lock(mtx);
        // Only work that needs the lock
    }
    // Do non-critical work here
}
```

4. Optimizing Performance in Concurrent Applications

Performance optimization is a key aspect of developing efficient concurrent applications. Here are some strategies to enhance performance.

4.1 Measure and Profile Performance

Before optimizing, always measure performance using profiling tools to identify bottlenecks. This will help you focus your optimization efforts on the most critical areas.

Tools for Profiling:

- **gprof**: For call graph profiling and function execution times.
- **Valgrind**: For memory profiling and leak detection.
- **Visual Studio Profiler**: For integrated profiling in Microsoft Visual Studio.

4.2 Reduce Context Switching

Excessive context switching can degrade performance. To minimize context switches:

- Limit the number of active threads to match the number of CPU cores.
- Use a thread pool to manage a fixed number of threads that can be reused for different tasks.

Example: Using a Thread Pool

```cpp
Copy code
class ThreadPool {
    // Implementation of a thread pool to manage thread reuse
};
```

4.3 Optimize Locking Strategies

Consider the following strategies to optimize locking in your applications:

- **Use Fine-Grained Locking**: Protect smaller sections of code with separate locks to reduce contention.
- **Avoid Locking for Read Operations**: Use shared locks for read-heavy operations to allow concurrent reads.

Example: Using Shared Mutex for Reader-Writer

```cpp
Copy code
std::shared_mutex rwMutex;  // Shared mutex for concurrent reads

void readData() {
    std::shared_lock<std::shared_mutex> lock(rwMutex);
    // Read shared data
}
```

5. Ensuring Thread Safety

Thread safety is crucial for preventing race conditions and ensuring consistent state across threads. Here are some best practices for maintaining thread safety.

5.1 Design for Thread Safety

When designing your classes and functions, consider thread safety from the outset:

- **Encapsulate Shared State**: Use private data members and provide public methods for access to avoid direct manipulation of shared data.
- **Immutable Data Structures**: Use immutable data structures whenever possible to prevent accidental modifications by multiple threads.

Example: Encapsulation of Shared State

```cpp
Copy code
class SafeCounter {
public:
    void increment() {
        std::lock_guard<std::mutex> lock(mtx);
        ++count;
    }

    int getCount() {
        std::lock_guard<std::mutex> lock(mtx);
        return count;
    }
private:
    int count = 0;
    std::mutex mtx;
};
```

5.2 Use Thread-Local Storage

Thread-local storage allows you to create variables that are unique to each thread, preventing data from being shared inadvertently.

Example: Using thread_local

```cpp
Copy code
thread_local int threadSpecificData = 0;  // Each thread has its own copy
```

```
void threadFunction() {
    threadSpecificData++;
    std::cout << "Thread-specific data: " << threadSpecificData <<
    std::endl;
}
```

6. Testing and Debugging Concurrent Applications

Testing and debugging multithreaded applications can be challenging due to the non-deterministic nature of thread execution. Here are some strategies to effectively test and debug concurrent code.

6.1 Use Stress Testing

Stress testing involves running your application under heavy load to identify concurrency issues such as race conditions, deadlocks, and performance bottlenecks. This can be achieved by simulating many threads accessing shared resources concurrently.

Example: Stress Testing with Multiple Threads

cpp
Copy code
```
void stressTest() {
    std::vector<std::thread> threads;
    for (int i = 0; i < 100; ++i) {
        threads.emplace_back([] { /* Perform operations here */ });
    }
    for (auto& t : threads) {
        t.join();
    }
}
```

6.2 Employ Debugging Tools

Utilize debugging tools specifically designed for multithreaded applications:

- **ThreadSanitizer**: A tool that detects data races and other threading issues.
- **Valgrind's Helgrind**: A tool for detecting synchronization errors in multithreaded C/C++ programs.

6.3 Logging and Monitoring

Implement logging and monitoring in your applications to track the behavior of threads and identify potential issues. Use logging to output thread states, synchronization events, and error messages.

Example: Simple Logging

```cpp
Copy code
#include <iostream>
#include <mutex>

std::mutex logMutex;

void log(const std::string& message) {
    std::lock_guard<std::mutex> lock(logMutex);
    std::cout << message << std::endl;
}
```

7. Conclusion

In this chapter, we explored best practices and design guidelines for C++ concurrency. We covered essential topics, including:

- Structuring concurrent code for clarity and maintainability.
- Managing resources and synchronization effectively.
- Optimizing performance while ensuring thread safety.
- Testing and debugging multithreaded applications.

By following these best practices, you will be better equipped to design and implement robust, high-performance concurrent applications in C++. As you continue to develop your skills in C++ concurrency, remember that the key to success lies in balancing complexity with performance, ensuring that your applications are both efficient and maintainable.

8. Looking Ahead

As you move forward in your journey with C++ concurrency, stay informed about emerging trends, tools, and best practices. The landscape of software development is continually evolving, and keeping up with the latest advancements will ensure that your skills remain relevant and effective. By embracing a culture of learning and experimentation, you will be well-prepared to tackle the challenges of concurrent programming in the years to come.

In the next chapter, we will wrap up the book with final thoughts, reflections on the journey through C++ concurrency, and a look at future developments in the field.

Chapter 12: The Future of Concurrency in C++

As we stand on the brink of new technological advancements, the field of concurrency in C++ continues to evolve. This chapter will explore the future of concurrency, emerging trends, and anticipated developments in the C++ language and its libraries. We will delve into the implications of these advancements on software development practices, performance optimization, and the overall landscape of multithreaded programming.

1. Introduction to the Future of Concurrency

The landscape of concurrency in programming is rapidly changing, driven by advancements in hardware, software paradigms, and the increasing demand for responsive, high-performance applications. This chapter will address the following key areas:

- **Emerging Trends in C++ Concurrency**: Explore the latest trends shaping the future of concurrency in C++.
- **Technological Advancements**: Discuss the impact of hardware developments on concurrent programming.
- **C++ Language Evolution**: Examine how future C++ standards may

influence concurrency features and practices.
- **Best Practices for Future Development**: Offer guidelines to prepare for future developments in C++ concurrency.

2. Emerging Trends in C++ Concurrency

2.1 Asynchronous Programming and Coroutines

The adoption of asynchronous programming models has become increasingly popular in modern software development. With the introduction of coroutines in C++20, developers can write asynchronous code that is more intuitive and easier to read. Coroutines allow functions to be paused and resumed, enabling more efficient use of resources without blocking threads.

Example of Coroutines:

```cpp
Copy code
#include <iostream>
#include <coroutine>
#include <thread>
#include <chrono>

struct Task {
    struct promise_type {
        Task get_return_object() { return {}; }
        std::suspend_never initial_suspend() { return {}; }
        std::suspend_never final_suspend() noexcept { return {}; }
        void unhandled_exception() {}
        void return_void() {}
    };
};

Task asyncOperation() {
    std::cout << "Starting operation...\n";
    std::this_thread::sleep_for(std::chrono::seconds(2)); // Simulate work
    std::cout << "Operation complete!\n";
}
```

```cpp
int main() {
    asyncOperation();
    std::cout << "Main function continues...\n";
    return 0;
}
```

In this example, coroutines allow for more straightforward management of asynchronous tasks. As the language evolves, we can expect coroutines to become a standard approach for handling concurrency in C++.

2.2 Increased Focus on Parallel Algorithms

The C++ Standard Library has increasingly incorporated parallel algorithms, which allow developers to express parallelism at a higher level of abstraction. These algorithms make it easier to leverage multicore processors without delving into the complexities of thread management.

Example of Parallel Algorithms:

```cpp
Copy code
#include <iostream>
#include <vector>
#include <numeric>
#include <execution>

int main() {
    std::vector<int> data(1000000, 1);
    int sum = std::reduce(std::execution::par, data.begin(),
    data.end(), 0);
    std::cout << "Sum: " << sum << std::endl;
    return 0;
}
```

In this example, the std::reduce algorithm is executed in parallel, utilizing the available CPU cores effectively. Future standards are expected to expand the range of parallel algorithms available in C++.

3. Technological Advancements Impacting Concurrency

3.1 Advancements in Hardware

The continued development of hardware architectures, particularly multi-core processors, has a significant impact on how concurrency is approached in software. As the number of cores on processors increases, developers must find efficient ways to utilize these resources.

Key Hardware Trends:

- **Increased Core Counts**: Modern processors with many cores require effective strategies for distributing workloads.
- **Heterogeneous Computing**: The rise of GPUs and specialized hardware (like TPUs) necessitates new approaches for parallel processing.
- **Memory Architectures**: Advances in memory technologies (e.g., DDR5, HBM) can reduce latency and improve data access times for concurrent applications.

3.2 Development of Multi-threaded Libraries

The growth of libraries and frameworks that facilitate multithreading will continue to shape the future of concurrency in C++. Libraries such as Intel Threading Building Blocks (TBB), OpenMP, and Boost provide abstractions that simplify concurrent programming, making it easier for developers to write high-performance applications.

Example of Intel TBB:

```cpp
Copy code
#include <tbb/tbb.h>
#include <iostream>
#include <vector>

int main() {
    std::vector<int> data(1000000, 1);
    int sum =
```

```
    tbb::parallel_reduce(tbb::blocked_range<int*>(data.data(),
    data.data() + data.size()),
                                0,
                                [](const
                                tbb::blocked_range<int*>& r,
                                int init) {
                                    for (int* p = r.begin(); p
                                    != r.end(); ++p) init += *p;
                                    return init;
                                },
                                std::plus<int>());
    std::cout << "Sum: " << sum << std::endl;
    return 0;
}
```

In this example, Intel TBB simplifies the process of parallel reduction, allowing for better utilization of available cores.

4. C++ Language Evolution and Its Impact on Concurrency

The evolution of the C++ language itself will continue to influence how concurrency is approached in future applications. As new standards are developed, features that simplify concurrency and enhance safety will be introduced.

4.1 Future C++ Standards

The C++ standards committee is actively working on improvements and new features that will influence concurrency. Some potential features include:

- **Pattern Matching**: Streamlining decision-making processes can reduce complexity in concurrent applications.
- **Enhanced Memory Models**: Further refinements in the memory model can provide developers with more control over memory visibility in multithreaded environments.
- **Expanded Library Support**: Anticipated enhancements to standard libraries will include more robust concurrency features and tools for

managing parallelism.

5. Best Practices for Future Development in C++ Concurrency

As concurrency evolves, so too should the best practices for managing it. Here are some recommendations for developers to prepare for the future of C++ concurrency:

5.1 Embrace Modern C++ Features

Utilize features introduced in C++11 and later, such as lambda expressions, smart pointers, and range-based loops, to simplify code and enhance readability. Keeping up with modern practices ensures that your code remains relevant and maintainable.

Example of Using Lambda Expressions:

```cpp
Copy code
#include <iostream>
#include <vector>
#include <algorithm>

int main() {
    std::vector<int> data = {1, 2, 3, 4, 5};
    std::for_each(data.begin(), data.end(), [](int& n) { n *= 2;
});
    for (const auto& n : data) std::cout << n << " ";   // Output: 2 4 6 8 10
    return 0;
}
```

In this example, lambda expressions make the code concise and expressive.

5.2 Continuously Profile and Optimize

Regular profiling of applications is essential to identify performance bottlenecks and optimize resource usage. Adopt a proactive approach to performance analysis, using profiling tools to gather data on thread behavior, memory usage, and execution times.

5.3 Engage with the Community

Participate in forums, open-source projects, and conferences to stay connected with developments in C++ concurrency. Engaging with the community provides opportunities to learn from others, share knowledge, and collaborate on innovative solutions.

6. Conclusion

The future of concurrency in C++ holds exciting possibilities as the language evolves and technology advances. This chapter discussed key trends in concurrency, technological developments, and the impact of future C++ standards on concurrent programming.

By embracing modern C++ features, continuously profiling and optimizing your applications, and engaging with the community, you can navigate the challenges and opportunities of C++ concurrency effectively. As you continue your journey in this field, remember that the landscape of concurrency is dynamic, and staying informed will be crucial for your success in developing high-performance, concurrent applications.

In the next chapter, we will provide final reflections on the journey through C++ concurrency, summarize key takeaways, and offer guidance for future exploration in this critical area of software development.

Chapter 13: Reflections and Future Directions in C++ Concurrency

As we reach the final chapter of this exploration into C++ concurrency, it's essential to reflect on what we have learned, the evolution of multithreading practices, and the future directions in the field. This chapter aims to summarize the key concepts discussed throughout the book, address the challenges faced by developers, and provide insights into emerging trends that will shape the future of concurrency in C++ programming.

1. Recap of Key Concepts

Throughout this book, we have navigated the multifaceted landscape of concurrency in C++. We began with foundational concepts and gradually progressed to advanced topics and real-world applications. Below is a summary of the key concepts covered:

1.1 Concurrency vs. Parallelism

Understanding the distinction between concurrency and parallelism was critical to our journey. Concurrency allows multiple tasks to make progress without necessarily running simultaneously, while parallelism involves executing multiple tasks at the same time.

1.2 C++ Concurrency Support

C++ provides robust support for concurrency through its standard library, which includes:

- **<thread>**: For creating and managing threads.
- **<mutex>**: For synchronization, allowing safe access to shared resources.
- **<condition_variable>**: For signaling between threads, enabling coordinated operations.
- **<future>**: For asynchronous programming, allowing threads to retrieve results from tasks running in the background.

1.3 Synchronization Mechanisms

We explored various synchronization mechanisms to prevent race conditions and ensure data integrity. Key mechanisms include:

- **Mutexes**: Used for exclusive access to shared resources.
- **Condition Variables**: Used to wait for specific conditions before proceeding.
- **Atomic Operations**: Lightweight mechanisms for managing simple shared variables.

1.4 Concurrency Design Patterns

We discussed several concurrency design patterns, including:

- **Producer-Consumer**: Managing the flow of data between producers and consumers.
- **Reader-Writer**: Allowing multiple readers or a single writer access to shared resources.

- **Future and Promise**: Facilitating asynchronous operations and handling results.

1.5 Advanced Topics in Performance Optimization

We delved into performance tuning and optimization strategies, focusing on minimizing lock contention, efficient thread usage, and cache optimization. Additionally, we emphasized the importance of measuring and profiling applications to identify bottlenecks.

1.6 Best Practices for Concurrent Programming

Key best practices included:

- Keeping code simple and maintainable.
- Managing resources effectively using RAII (Resource Acquisition Is Initialization).
- Designing for thread safety from the outset.
- Employing stress testing and debugging tools to identify and resolve issues.

2. Challenges in C++ Concurrency

While concurrency in C++ offers significant advantages, it also introduces challenges that developers must navigate. Here, we reflect on some of these challenges:

2.1 Complexity of Multithreaded Code

Concurrency can significantly increase the complexity of code. Writing multithreaded applications requires careful management of thread lifecycles, synchronization, and shared data access. This complexity can lead to bugs and unintended behaviors if not handled correctly.

2.2 Race Conditions and Deadlocks

Race conditions occur when multiple threads access shared data simultaneously, leading to inconsistent results. Deadlocks occur when two or more threads are waiting for each other to release resources, causing the program to hang. Detecting and resolving these issues can be particularly challenging.

2.3 Debugging Multithreaded Applications

Debugging multithreaded applications is often more complicated than debugging single-threaded programs. Issues like race conditions may not manifest consistently, making them difficult to reproduce and fix.

2.4 Performance Trade-offs

While concurrency can improve performance, improper use can lead to performance degradation. Excessive locking can introduce bottlenecks, and too many threads can lead to increased context switching, which negatively impacts overall application performance.

3. The Evolving Landscape of C++ Concurrency

As we look to the future of concurrency in C++, several trends and advancements are shaping the landscape. This section explores these developments and their potential implications for developers.

3.1 Ongoing Language Improvements

The C++ language is continually evolving, with each new standard introducing features that enhance concurrency support. Recent advancements, such as the introduction of coroutines in C++20, provide developers with more intuitive and efficient ways to handle asynchronous programming. As the language evolves, we can expect even more enhancements that will streamline concurrency.

3.2 Growing Use of Parallel Algorithms

The adoption of parallel algorithms in the C++ Standard Library has become increasingly common. These algorithms enable developers to express parallelism at a higher level of abstraction, allowing them to leverage multicore processors effectively. Future C++ standards are expected to expand the range of parallel algorithms available, making it easier for developers to optimize their applications.

3.3 Enhanced Tooling for Concurrency

The development of advanced profiling and debugging tools continues to improve the ability to analyze and optimize concurrent applications. Tools that provide insights into thread behavior, resource usage, and performance metrics are essential for developing robust concurrent systems. Expect further advancements in tools that simplify debugging and profiling of multithreaded applications.

3.4 Emphasis on Functional Programming Paradigms

The influence of functional programming paradigms is growing in C++. Concepts such as immutability and higher-order functions can help reduce side effects and make concurrent programming easier. This trend is likely to continue, leading to the adoption of more functional programming principles in C++.

4. Recommendations for Future Development

As we look ahead, here are some recommendations for developers to effectively navigate the evolving landscape of C++ concurrency:

4.1 Embrace Modern C++ Features

Utilize features introduced in C++11 and later, such as lambda expressions, smart pointers, and range-based loops, to simplify code and enhance readability. Keeping up with modern practices ensures that your code remains relevant and maintainable.

4.2 Stay Informed about Emerging Trends

Continuously educate yourself about new developments in C++ concurrency, including language features, libraries, and best practices. Engage with the community through forums, blogs, and conferences to stay informed about emerging trends.

4.3 Regularly Profile and Optimize Applications

Regular profiling of applications is essential to identify performance bottlenecks and optimize resource usage. Adopt a proactive approach to performance analysis, using profiling tools to gather data on thread behavior, memory usage, and execution times.

4.4 Utilize Existing Libraries and Frameworks

Take advantage of existing libraries and frameworks that offer robust concurrency features. Libraries such as Intel TBB, OpenMP, and Boost provide powerful abstractions for managing concurrency and parallelism, saving you time and effort in implementing low-level concurrency mechanisms.

4.5 Test Rigorously for Concurrency Issues

Implement thorough testing strategies that include stress testing, race condition detection, and deadlock analysis. Use tools specifically designed for multithreaded applications, such as ThreadSanitizer and Valgrind, to identify and resolve concurrency issues.

5. Conclusion

In this final chapter, we reflected on the journey through C++ concurrency, summarizing key concepts, challenges, and emerging trends. We discussed the ongoing evolution of the C++ language, the growing importance of parallel algorithms, and the advancements in tooling for concurrent programming.

By embracing modern C++ features, staying informed about emerging trends, and adopting best practices, developers can successfully navigate the complexities of concurrency. The future of C++ concurrency is bright, with many opportunities for innovation and improvement.

As you move forward in your journey with C++ concurrency, remember that the landscape is dynamic and ever-changing. The skills you have developed throughout this book will serve you well as you tackle new challenges and explore the exciting possibilities that concurrency has to offer in your projects.

In conclusion, concurrency in C++ is not just a technical skill; it is a mindset that enables you to create responsive, efficient, and scalable applications. As you continue to learn and grow in this field, embrace the challenges and opportunities that concurrency presents, and let your creativity drive your innovations in software development.

Chapter 14: Case Studies and Applications of C++ Concurrency

In this chapter, we will explore real-world case studies and applications that exemplify the power and utility of concurrency in C++. We will analyze various domains where multithreading and parallel processing are applied to enhance performance, responsiveness, and scalability. Each case study will provide insights into the design decisions made, the challenges faced, and the best practices employed in implementing concurrent solutions.

1. Introduction to Case Studies in C++ Concurrency

Concurrency is a critical aspect of modern software development, enabling applications to leverage the full potential of multicore processors. This chapter presents a range of case studies that demonstrate how C++ concurrency is applied in practical scenarios, including:

- A financial trading system.
- A web server handling multiple requests.
- A video processing application.
- A scientific simulation.

By examining these examples, we will gain valuable insights into the practical implementation of concurrency concepts and design patterns discussed throughout the book.

2. Case Study 1: Financial Trading System

2.1 Overview of the Financial Trading System

The financial trading system is designed to process real-time market data, execute trades, and manage user accounts concurrently. It must handle thousands of transactions per second while ensuring data integrity and responsiveness. The primary components of this system include:

- **Market Data Handler**: Receives and processes real-time market data.
- **Order Management System (OMS)**: Manages buy and sell orders.
- **Risk Management**: Evaluates the risk of open positions.
- **User Interface**: Allows users to interact with the system.

2.2 Designing the Financial Trading System

2.2.1 Market Data Handler

The market data handler is responsible for receiving real-time data from exchanges and distributing it to other components of the system. Given the high volume of incoming data, this component must be designed for high throughput and low latency.

Example of Market Data Handler Implementation:

```cpp
Copy code
#include <iostream>
#include <thread>
#include <mutex>
#include <queue>
#include <condition_variable>
```

```cpp
std::queue<std::string> marketDataQueue;
std::mutex queueMutex;
std::condition_variable dataAvailable;

void marketDataReceiver() {
    while (true) {
        // Simulate receiving market data
        std::this_thread::sleep_for(std::chrono::milliseconds(100));
        std::string data = "Market data";  // Replace with actual
        data

        {
            std::lock_guard<std::mutex> lock(queueMutex);
            marketDataQueue.push(data);
        }

        dataAvailable.notify_one();  // Notify data processors
    }
}

void processMarketData() {
    while (true) {
        std::string data;
        {
            std::unique_lock<std::mutex> lock(queueMutex);
            dataAvailable.wait(lock, [] { return
            !marketDataQueue.empty(); });

            data = marketDataQueue.front();
            marketDataQueue.pop();
        }

        // Process market data
        std::cout << "Processing: " << data << std::endl;
    }
}

int main() {
    std::thread receiver(marketDataReceiver);
    std::thread processor(processMarketData);
```

```
    receiver.join();
    processor.join();

    return 0;
}
```

In this implementation, the market data receiver simulates receiving data and pushes it onto a queue. The data processor waits for data to be available and processes it as soon as it arrives.

2.2.2 Order Management System (OMS)

The OMS handles buy and sell orders from users. It must ensure that orders are executed quickly and accurately while managing user accounts.

Example of Order Management System Implementation:

```cpp
Copy code
#include <iostream>
#include <thread>
#include <mutex>
#include <unordered_map>

std::unordered_map<std::string, double> userAccounts;  // User
account balances
std::mutex accountMutex;

void executeOrder(const std::string& userId, double amount) {
    std::lock_guard<std::mutex> lock(accountMutex);
    userAccounts[userId] += amount;   // Update user balance
    std::cout << "Executed order for " << userId << ", new
    balance: " << userAccounts[userId] << std::endl;
}
```

In this example, the executeOrder function updates the user's balance while ensuring thread safety using a mutex.

2.3 Performance Considerations

In a financial trading system, performance is crucial. Considerations include:

- **Latency**: Minimize latency by optimizing data processing and order execution.
- **Throughput**: Ensure high throughput by processing multiple orders and market data concurrently.
- **Fault Tolerance**: Implement mechanisms to handle failures gracefully, ensuring data integrity and continuity of service.

3. Case Study 2: Web Server Handling Multiple Requests

3.1 Overview of the Web Server

The web server is designed to handle multiple client requests concurrently, serving static and dynamic content. The primary responsibilities include:

- Listening for incoming connections.
- Handling HTTP requests and serving responses.
- Managing a pool of worker threads to process requests concurrently.

3.2 Designing the Web Server

3.2.1 Server Loop

The server loop listens for incoming connections and spawns worker threads to handle each request.

Example of Web Server Implementation:

```cpp
Copy code
#include <iostream>
#include <thread>
```

CHAPTER 14: CASE STUDIES AND APPLICATIONS OF C++ CONCURRENCY

```cpp
#include <vector>
#include <queue>
#include <mutex>
#include <condition_variable>
#include <cstring>
#include <arpa/inet.h>
#include <unistd.h>

std::queue<int> requestQueue;     // Queue for client sockets
std::mutex queueMutex;            // Mutex for synchronizing access
to the queue
std::condition_variable cv;       // Condition variable for
signaling
bool serverRunning = true;        // Flag to control the server loop

void handleRequest(int clientSocket) {
    char buffer[1024];
    std::memset(buffer, 0, sizeof(buffer));

    // Read the request from the client
    read(clientSocket, buffer, sizeof(buffer));
    std::cout << "Request received:\n" << buffer << std::endl;

    // Send a simple HTTP response
    const char* response = "HTTP/1.1 200 OK\r\nContent-Length:
    13\r\n\r\nHello, World!";
    write(clientSocket, response, strlen(response));

    close(clientSocket);
}

void serverLoop(int port) {
    int serverSocket, clientSocket;
    struct sockaddr_in serverAddr, clientAddr;
    socklen_t clientAddrLen = sizeof(clientAddr);

    // Create socket
    serverSocket = socket(AF_INET, SOCK_STREAM, 0);
    serverAddr.sin_family = AF_INET;
    serverAddr.sin_addr.s_addr = INADDR_ANY;
```

```cpp
        serverAddr.sin_port = htons(port);

        // Bind the socket
        bind(serverSocket, (struct sockaddr*)&serverAddr,
        sizeof(serverAddr));
        listen(serverSocket, 5);   // Listen for incoming connections

        std::cout << "Web server is listening on port " << port <<
        std::endl;

        while (serverRunning) {
            // Accept a client connection
            clientSocket = accept(serverSocket, (struct
            sockaddr*)&clientAddr, &clientAddrLen);

            {
                std::lock_guard<std::mutex> lock(queueMutex);
                requestQueue.push(clientSocket);
            }

            cv.notify_one();   // Notify a waiting worker thread
        }

        close(serverSocket);
    }

    void workerThread() {
        while (true) {
            int clientSocket;

            {
                std::unique_lock<std::mutex> lock(queueMutex);
                cv.wait(lock, [] { return !requestQueue.empty() ||
                !serverRunning; });
                if (!serverRunning && requestQueue.empty()) break;

                clientSocket = requestQueue.front();
                requestQueue.pop();
            }
```

```cpp
            handleRequest(clientSocket);    // Process the request
        }
    }

    int main() {
        const int numWorkers = 4;
        std::vector<std::thread> workers;

        for (int i = 0; i < numWorkers; ++i) {
            workers.emplace_back(workerThread);    // Start worker
            threads
        }

        serverLoop(8080);    // Start the server loop on port 8080

        // Shutdown logic to gracefully stop the server can be added
        here

        for (auto& worker : workers) {
            worker.join();    // Wait for worker threads to finish
        }

        return 0;
    }
```

In this implementation:

- The server listens for incoming connections and adds client sockets to a request queue.
- Worker threads process the requests from the queue, ensuring concurrent handling of client connections.

3.3 Performance Considerations

For a web server, performance optimization is critical. Key considerations include:

- **Concurrency Model**: Choose an appropriate concurrency model (e.g., thread pool) to manage multiple connections efficiently.
- **Request Handling**: Optimize request processing to minimize latency.
- **Scalability**: Design the server to scale effectively with increasing user load.

4. Case Study 3: Video Processing Application

4.1 Overview of the Video Processing Application

The video processing application is designed to process video files for various operations, such as encoding, decoding, and applying effects. Given the computational intensity of video processing tasks, concurrency is essential for achieving efficient performance. The main components of the application include:

- **Video Reader**: Reads video frames from input files.
- **Frame Processor**: Applies effects or transformations to individual frames.
- **Video Writer**: Writes processed frames to output files.

4.2 Designing the Video Processing Application

4.2.1 Frame Processing Pipeline

The application follows a pipeline architecture, where each component processes video data in parallel.

Example of Video Processing Pipeline Implementation:

```cpp
Copy code
#include <iostream>
#include <thread>
#include <vector>
```

```cpp
#include <queue>
#include <mutex>
#include <condition_variable>

std::queue<int> frameQueue;    // Queue for video frames
std::mutex queueMutex;         // Mutex for synchronizing access to the queue
std::condition_variable cv;    // Condition variable for signaling
bool processing = true;        // Flag to control the processing loop

void processFrame(int frameNumber) {
    // Simulate frame processing (e.g., apply effects)
    std::cout << "Processing frame: " << frameNumber << std::endl;
    std::this_thread::sleep_for(std::chrono::milliseconds(100));
    // Simulate processing time
}

void frameProducer() {
    for (int i = 0; i < 10; ++i) {
        {
            std::lock_guard<std::mutex> lock(queueMutex);
            frameQueue.push(i);   // Add frame to the queue
        }
        cv.notify_one();   // Notify a waiting consumer
        std::this_thread::sleep_for(std::chrono::milliseconds(50));
         // Simulate time between frames
    }
}

void frameConsumer() {
    while (processing || !frameQueue.empty()) {
        int frameNumber;
        {
            std::unique_lock<std::mutex> lock(queueMutex);
            cv.wait(lock, [] { return !frameQueue.empty() || !processing; });
            if (!processing && frameQueue.empty()) break;

            frameNumber = frameQueue.front();
```

```cpp
            frameQueue.pop();
        }

        processFrame(frameNumber);   // Process the frame
    }
}

int main() {
    std::thread producer(frameProducer);   // Start the frame
    producer
    const int numConsumers = 4;
    std::vector<std::thread> consumers;

    for (int i = 0; i < numConsumers; ++i) {
        consumers.emplace_back(frameConsumer);   // Start consumer
        threads
    }

    producer.join();   // Wait for the producer to finish
    processing = false;   // Stop processing

    cv.notify_all();   // Notify all consumers to exit

    for (auto& consumer : consumers) {
        consumer.join();   // Wait for consumer threads to finish
    }

    return 0;
}
```

In this example:

- The frame producer simulates reading video frames and adds them to a queue.
- Multiple consumer threads process frames concurrently, ensuring efficient handling of video data.

4.3 Performance Considerations

Key performance considerations for the video processing application include:

- **Parallel Processing**: Utilize multiple threads to process frames concurrently, reducing overall processing time.
- **Load Balancing**: Ensure that the workload is evenly distributed among consumer threads to maximize resource utilization.
- **Resource Management**: Manage resources effectively to avoid bottlenecks in reading or writing video data.

5. Case Study 4: Scientific Simulation

5.1 Overview of the Scientific Simulation

Scientific simulations often require the processing of large datasets and complex calculations. This case study will demonstrate how concurrency can be leveraged to speed up simulations in a scientific computing application.

5.2 Designing the Scientific Simulation

5.2.1 Simulation of Particle Dynamics

The scientific simulation will model the dynamics of particles interacting in a three-dimensional space. The primary components of the application include:

- **Particle Data Structure**: Represents individual particles with their positions, velocities, and forces.
- **Simulation Engine**: Computes the interactions between particles and updates their states.
- **Result Visualization**: Displays the results of the simulation in real-time.

Example of Particle Dynamics Simulation Implementation:

C++ FOR CONCURRENCY AND PARALLEL PROGRAMMING

```cpp
Copy code
#include <iostream>
#include <vector>
#include <thread>
#include <mutex>
#include <random>

struct Particle {
    double x, y, z;    // Position
    double vx, vy, vz; // Velocity
};

std::vector<Particle> particles(1000);  // Vector of particles
std::mutex particleMutex;  // Mutex for synchronizing access to particles

void updateParticles(int start, int end) {
    for (int i = start; i < end; ++i) {
        // Update particle positions based on their velocities
        {
            std::lock_guard<std::mutex> lock(particleMutex);
            particles[i].x += particles[i].vx;
            particles[i].y += particles[i].vy;
            particles[i].z += particles[i].vz;
        }
    }
}

int main() {
    const int numParticles = particles.size();
    const int numThreads = 4;
    std::vector<std::thread> threads;

    // Initialize particles with random positions and velocities
    std::random_device rd;
    std::mt19937 gen(rd());
    std::uniform_real_distribution<> dis(0.0, 1.0);
```

```cpp
    for (auto& particle : particles) {
        particle.x = dis(gen);
        particle.y = dis(gen);
        particle.z = dis(gen);
        particle.vx = dis(gen) * 0.1;  // Random velocity
        particle.vy = dis(gen) * 0.1;
        particle.vz = dis(gen) * 0.1;
    }

    int chunkSize = numParticles / numThreads;

    // Start threads to update particle positions
    for (int i = 0; i < numThreads; ++i) {
        int start = i * chunkSize;
        int end = (i == numThreads - 1) ? numParticles : start + chunkSize;
        threads.emplace_back(updateParticles, start, end);
    }

    // Wait for all threads to finish
    for (auto& t : threads) {
        t.join();
    }

    // Display updated particle positions
    for (const auto& particle : particles) {
        std::cout << "Particle Position: (" << particle.x << ", "
        << particle.y << ", " << particle.z << ")" << std::endl;
    }

    return 0;
}
```

In this example:

- The simulation initializes a set of particles with random positions and velocities.
- Multiple threads update the positions of the particles concurrently, demonstrating the parallel processing of calculations.

5.3 Performance Considerations

Key considerations for optimizing the scientific simulation include:

- **Granularity of Updates**: Balance the workload across threads to avoid some threads finishing early while others are still busy.
- **Synchronization Overhead**: Minimize the use of locks to reduce contention and improve performance.
- **Data Locality**: Organize particle data to improve cache performance and reduce memory access latency.

6. Conclusion

In this chapter, we explored several case studies that illustrate the practical application of C++ concurrency. We examined a financial trading system, a web server handling multiple requests, a video processing application, and a scientific simulation. Each case study highlighted the design decisions made, the challenges faced, and the performance considerations taken into account.

By understanding these real-world applications, you can gain valuable insights into the effective implementation of concurrency in your projects. The knowledge gained from these examples will equip you to tackle your own concurrency challenges in C++ programming.

In the next chapter, we will wrap up the book with final thoughts on the journey through C++ concurrency, summarizing key takeaways, and offering guidance for future exploration in this critical area of software development.

Chapter 15: Final Reflections and the Future of C++ Concurrency

As we conclude our comprehensive exploration of C++ concurrency, it is essential to reflect on the journey we've undertaken. In this final chapter, we will summarize the key learnings, highlight the challenges faced by developers in concurrent programming, and look ahead at the future of concurrency in C++. This chapter will also offer practical advice for developers looking to enhance their skills in this vital area of software development.

1. Recap of Key Learnings

Over the course of this book, we have covered a wide array of topics related to C++ concurrency. From foundational concepts to advanced techniques, the journey has provided you with a solid understanding of how to effectively implement concurrency in C++. Here are some key takeaways:

1.1 Understanding Concurrency and Parallelism

We began by distinguishing between concurrency and parallelism. Understanding these concepts is crucial for designing applications that efficiently utilize multicore processors.

- **Concurrency** involves managing multiple tasks at the same time, while not necessarily executing them simultaneously.
- **Parallelism** involves executing multiple tasks at the exact same time, typically on different cores.

1.2 C++ Concurrency Support

C++ offers robust support for concurrency through its standard libraries introduced in C++11. These include:

- **std::thread**: Facilitates the creation and management of threads.
- **std::mutex and std::lock_guard**: Provide synchronization mechanisms to prevent race conditions.
- **std::condition_variable**: Allows threads to wait for specific conditions.
- **std::future and std::promise**: Enable asynchronous programming by providing mechanisms to retrieve results from background tasks.

1.3 Synchronization and Thread Safety

We explored various synchronization techniques, emphasizing the importance of thread safety in concurrent applications. Key mechanisms included:

- **Mutexes**: To protect shared resources from concurrent access.
- **Condition Variables**: For signaling between threads, allowing for coordinated execution.
- **Atomic Operations**: For lightweight, lock-free management of shared variables.

1.4 Performance Optimization

Performance optimization is a critical aspect of developing concurrent applications. We discussed techniques to enhance performance, including:

CHAPTER 15: FINAL REFLECTIONS AND THE FUTURE OF C++...

- Minimizing lock contention and reducing the scope of locks.
- Using thread pools to manage threads efficiently.
- Implementing parallel algorithms to leverage multicore processors effectively.

1.5 Best Practices for Concurrent Programming

We reviewed best practices that guide developers in writing robust, maintainable, and efficient concurrent code, including:

- Structuring code for clarity and simplicity.
- Employing RAII (Resource Acquisition Is Initialization) for resource management.
- Thorough testing and profiling of concurrent applications.

2. Challenges in C++ Concurrency

While C++ concurrency offers powerful tools and capabilities, it also presents challenges that developers must navigate. Reflecting on these challenges can provide valuable insights into the complexities of concurrent programming.

2.1 Complexity of Multithreaded Code

Writing concurrent code inherently increases complexity. Managing multiple threads, ensuring correct synchronization, and maintaining shared state can lead to confusion and bugs. Developers must adopt a disciplined approach to design and code organization to mitigate these complexities.

2.2 Race Conditions and Deadlocks

Race conditions occur when multiple threads access shared data simultaneously, leading to unpredictable behavior. Deadlocks happen when two or more threads are waiting for each other to release resources, causing the program to halt. Detecting and resolving these issues requires careful design and thorough testing.

2.3 Debugging Multithreaded Applications

Debugging multithreaded applications can be particularly challenging due to the non-deterministic nature of thread execution. Issues such as race conditions may not manifest consistently, making them difficult to reproduce and fix. Developers need to employ specialized tools and techniques for debugging concurrency issues.

2.4 Performance Trade-offs

While concurrency can improve performance, improper use can lead to performance degradation. For instance, excessive locking can introduce bottlenecks, and having too many threads can lead to increased context switching, adversely affecting performance. Balancing concurrency with performance requires careful consideration and profiling.

3. The Evolving Landscape of C++ Concurrency

The field of concurrency in C++ is continually evolving, driven by advancements in technology and changes in programming paradigms. This section examines the trends and developments shaping the future of C++ concurrency.

3.1 Ongoing Improvements in C++

The C++ language is undergoing continuous evolution, with each new standard introducing features that enhance concurrency. The introduction of coroutines in C++20 exemplifies this evolution, allowing developers to write asynchronous code that is more intuitive and easier to manage.

3.2 Emphasis on Parallel Algorithms

The standardization of parallel algorithms within the C++ Standard Library has become increasingly prominent. These algorithms enable developers to express parallelism at a higher level of abstraction, allowing for easier and more effective utilization of multicore processors. Future standards are expected to expand the range of parallel algorithms, making concurrency more accessible.

3.3 Enhanced Tooling for Concurrency

The development of advanced profiling and debugging tools continues to improve the ability to analyze and optimize concurrent applications. Tools that provide insights into thread behavior, resource usage, and performance metrics are essential for developing robust concurrent systems. Expect further advancements in tooling that simplify debugging and profiling of multithreaded applications.

3.4 Functional Programming Paradigms

The influence of functional programming paradigms is growing in C++. Concepts such as immutability and higher-order functions can help reduce side effects and simplify concurrent programming. This trend may lead to the adoption of more functional programming principles within C++.

4. Recommendations for Future Development

As we look forward, here are several recommendations for developers to effectively navigate the evolving landscape of C++ concurrency:

4.1 Embrace Modern C++ Features

Utilize features introduced in C++11 and later, such as lambda expressions, smart pointers, and range-based loops, to simplify code and enhance readability. Keeping up with modern practices ensures that your code remains relevant and maintainable.

4.2 Stay Informed about Emerging Trends

Continuously educate yourself about new developments in C++ concurrency, including language features, libraries, and best practices. Engage with the community through forums, blogs, and conferences to stay informed about emerging trends.

4.3 Regularly Profile and Optimize Applications

Regular profiling of applications is essential to identify performance bottlenecks and optimize resource usage. Adopt a proactive approach to performance analysis, using profiling tools to gather data on thread behavior, memory usage, and execution times.

4.4 Utilize Existing Libraries and Frameworks

Take advantage of existing libraries and frameworks that offer robust concurrency features. Libraries such as Intel TBB, OpenMP, and Boost provide powerful abstractions for managing concurrency and parallelism, saving you time and effort in implementing low-level concurrency mechanisms.

4.5 Test Rigorously for Concurrency Issues

Implement thorough testing strategies that include stress testing, race condition detection, and deadlock analysis. Use tools specifically designed for multithreaded applications, such as ThreadSanitizer and Valgrind, to identify and resolve concurrency issues.

5. Final Thoughts

As we conclude this journey through C++ concurrency, it is clear that mastering concurrent programming is essential for building high-performance, responsive applications in today's multicore world. The key concepts, design patterns, and best practices discussed throughout this book provide a solid foundation for tackling the challenges of concurrency.

The future of concurrency in C++ holds exciting possibilities as the language continues to evolve and new technologies emerge. By embracing modern practices and staying informed about developments in the field, you can position yourself for success in the ever-changing landscape of software development.

5.1 Embrace the Journey Ahead

Concurrency is not just a technical skill; it is a mindset that enables you to create responsive, efficient, and scalable applications. As you continue to learn and grow in this field, embrace the challenges and opportunities that concurrency presents.

5.2 Encourage Collaboration and Knowledge Sharing

Engage with the C++ community to share your knowledge and learn from others. Contributing to open-source projects, participating in forums, and attending conferences can provide invaluable insights and foster collaboration.

5.3 Stay Curious and Experimental

The world of concurrency is dynamic, and staying curious will help you explore new ideas and approaches. Experiment with different concurrency models, libraries, and tools to expand your skill set and enhance your understanding.

5.4 Continue to Innovate

The applications of concurrency are vast, and as technology continues to advance, so too will the opportunities for innovation. Use your knowledge of C++ concurrency to tackle new challenges and create cutting-edge solutions in your projects.

6. Conclusion

In this final chapter, we have reflected on our journey through C++ concurrency, summarized the key learnings, and explored the future directions of concurrency in software development. The insights gained from this exploration will serve as a foundation for your continued growth in this critical area.

The world of concurrency in C++ is rich with possibilities, and as you move forward, remember that the skills you have developed will empower you to create robust, efficient, and scalable applications. Embrace the challenges, stay informed about emerging trends, and continue to innovate as you contribute to the exciting future of C++ concurrency.

With this concluding chapter, we hope to inspire you to embark on your journey in C++ concurrency, equipped with the knowledge and tools to make meaningful contributions to the world of software development.

Conclusion

As we reach the end of this comprehensive exploration into C++ concurrency, it's essential to reflect on the journey and the rich landscape we've traversed. The discussion of concurrency in C++ has not only covered the theoretical foundations but also provided practical insights and real-world applications. This conclusion aims to encapsulate the essence of what we have learned, the challenges we have faced, and the opportunities that lie ahead in the ever-evolving field of concurrent programming.

1. Key Takeaways

Throughout this book, we have highlighted several critical aspects of C++ concurrency that are crucial for any developer working in this area:

1.1 Fundamental Concepts

Understanding the foundational differences between concurrency and parallelism was paramount. Concurrency allows multiple tasks to progress simultaneously, which is essential in designing responsive applications, while parallelism focuses on executing multiple tasks at the same time. This differentiation helps guide developers in choosing the right strategies for their applications.

1.2 C++ Concurrency Features

The introduction of concurrency features in C++11 marked a significant advancement in the language. We explored the capabilities provided by the standard library, including:

- **std::thread** for managing threads.
- **std::mutex** and **std::lock_guard** for synchronization.
- **std::condition_variable** for signaling between threads.
- **std::future** and **std::promise** for managing asynchronous tasks.

These features empower developers to implement multithreading effectively and leverage the full potential of modern hardware.

1.3 Synchronization and Thread Safety

We emphasized the importance of thread safety and the mechanisms needed to ensure it. Effective synchronization strategies are vital to prevent race conditions, deadlocks, and data corruption. Key synchronization tools like mutexes, condition variables, and atomic operations were discussed extensively, providing developers with a toolkit to manage shared resources safely.

1.4 Performance Optimization Techniques

We explored various techniques for optimizing the performance of concurrent applications. Understanding how to minimize lock contention, utilize thread pools, and implement parallel algorithms can significantly enhance the responsiveness and efficiency of applications. The emphasis on profiling and testing ensures that performance is not just theoretical but practically achieved.

1.5 Best Practices for Concurrent Programming

The best practices shared throughout the book provide a roadmap for writing robust and maintainable concurrent code. Key recommendations include:

- Keeping code clear and concise to manage complexity.
- Utilizing RAII for resource management to prevent resource leaks.
- Engaging in rigorous testing and debugging to identify and resolve concurrency issues.

2. Challenges in Concurrent Programming

While C++ concurrency offers powerful tools and capabilities, it also presents challenges that require careful navigation:

2.1 Complexity

Concurrency adds complexity to code, making it imperative to adopt best practices in design and organization. Clear structuring of code and minimizing shared state are essential to reduce confusion and potential bugs.

2.2 Race Conditions and Deadlocks

Race conditions and deadlocks remain significant concerns in multi-threaded programming. Developers must be vigilant and implement proper synchronization techniques to avoid these issues, employing testing and debugging tools to identify problems early in the development process.

2.3 Debugging

The non-deterministic nature of thread execution can complicate debugging efforts. Specialized tools and techniques are necessary to effectively diagnose and resolve concurrency-related issues.

3. The Evolving Landscape of C++ Concurrency

The future of C++ concurrency is promising, with ongoing developments and trends that will shape how developers approach concurrent programming:

3.1 Language Improvements

The continuous evolution of the C++ language, particularly with recent standards, introduces features that simplify concurrent programming. The inclusion of coroutines in C++20 exemplifies this progress, allowing developers to write asynchronous code that is more intuitive.

3.2 Emphasis on Parallel Algorithms

The growing emphasis on parallel algorithms in the C++ Standard Library provides developers with higher-level abstractions for utilizing multicore processors. This trend makes it easier for developers to implement concurrency without delving into low-level threading details.

3.3 Enhanced Tools and Frameworks

The development of advanced profiling and debugging tools will continue to improve the ability to analyze and optimize concurrent applications. As tooling evolves, developers will have access to better resources for managing concurrency and performance.

3.4 Functional Programming Influence

The influence of functional programming paradigms is likely to grow, offering new ways to approach concurrency. Concepts such as immutability and higher-order functions can help reduce side effects and simplify concurrent code.

4. Recommendations for Future Development

As you move forward in your journey with C++ concurrency, consider the following recommendations:

4.1 Embrace Modern Practices

Stay current with modern C++ features and best practices. Embrace the advancements in the language and leverage them in your applications to write clearer, more efficient, and maintainable code.

4.2 Engage with the Community

Participate in discussions, forums, and open-source projects related to C++ concurrency. Engaging with the community will help you stay informed about new developments and best practices.

4.3 Experiment and Learn

Be proactive in experimenting with different concurrency models and techniques. Practical experience will deepen your understanding and help you find innovative solutions to concurrency challenges.

4.4 Regularly Profile Your Applications

Make performance profiling a regular part of your development process. Identifying and addressing bottlenecks early can prevent performance issues from becoming entrenched in your applications.

4.5 Test Thoroughly

Implement thorough testing strategies, including stress testing and concurrency testing. Use tools designed for multithreaded applications to catch issues before they reach production.

5. Final Thoughts

The journey through C++ concurrency has equipped you with a comprehensive understanding of the concepts, challenges, and best practices associated with multithreading. As technology continues to advance and the demands for high-performance applications grow, the importance of mastering concurrency cannot be overstated.

Concurrency is not just a set of techniques; it is a vital approach to building applications that can respond to user demands in real time while efficiently utilizing system resources. As you continue your exploration in this field, remember that the skills you have developed will empower you to create robust, efficient, and scalable applications.

The world of concurrency is dynamic, full of opportunities for innovation and improvement. Embrace the challenges, stay curious, and continue to learn as you navigate the exciting future of C++ concurrency. Your journey in this field is just beginning, and the possibilities are endless.

In conclusion, we hope that this book serves as a valuable resource for you, whether you are a beginner looking to understand the basics of concurrency or an experienced developer seeking to refine your skills. The knowledge you have gained will undoubtedly help you navigate the complexities of concurrent programming and contribute to your success in building high-performance C++ applications. Thank you for joining us on this journey through C++ concurrency!

www.ingramcontent.com/pod-product-compliance
Lightning Source LLC
Chambersburg PA
CBHW071025240526
45469CB00006BD/2096